The **Elephant** In The Room

The Elephant In The Room:
What Many See But Most Ignore

ISBN 978-1-160683-427-5

Published by Harrison House
Tulsa, OK 74145

Additional credit lines appear in "Notes" p. 247.

Developing Author: Robb Thompson
Project Manager: Justin Kane
Researcher: Erin Lashley
Editing/Proofreading: Karen Jahn
Cartoon Research: Linda Beck
Graphic Design: Amanda Fico
Cover Illustration & Chapter Title Page Illustrations: Juan Arevalo

Printed in the United States of America.

Contents

DEDICATION The most vital subjects of ethics and character have lived their existence on a sliding scale throughout the ages. This book is dedicated to those who, deep within, still believe that life, at its core, is made up of unchangeable absolutes. May these words be the stimulus that you need in order to be willing to stand for truth just one more day. These vital truths, written here, have been alive in a man whose life and accomplishments cause me to pen these words. His stand for truth, his love for character, and his example to the world are known in many circles. I further dedicate these words to Peter J. Daniels. If I achieve only half of his heart accomplishments, I will have lived a full life.

In my personal library, I have several thousand books that I consider to be the greatest material treasures I possess. But of all the books I own, the single greatest written work that has impacted my life is the book of Proverbs, written by Solomon. Very often, as I read the book of Proverbs, I think of Robb Thompson, whose life, sayings, and principles remind me so much of the truths found in this eternal book. In fact, in the margin next to Proverbs 16:23 (NLT) — "From a wise mind comes wise speech..." — I have written the name "Robb Thompson" because it makes me think of the incredible mind he possesses, the way he sees life, and his ability to interpret eternal principles in a way that enables me to live my life more wisely.

I've known Robb closely for more than two decades. Throughout these many years of friendship, I've seen him in various situations in life and have closely observed his actions and reactions to people and events. When it would have been easier to take the low road and thus avoid challenges with other people, I have seen Robb consistently take the high road to do what is right, even when it was difficult or, perhaps, what others deemed unnecessary. Robb simply refuses to veer from what he believes to be true.

As Robb's dear friend, I have seen his humanity and enjoyed his laughter, humor, and companionship. I have also shared moments with him when his heart has been torn or broken by a lack of integrity in others. Yet, in all the years of our friendship, I have never seen him surrender a principle he believed to be true, or fail to compassionately reach out to help those who have fallen or stumbled along the path of life. I have personally called upon Robb on several occasions, both as my friend and as a highly respected minister, to assist me through various situations in my life. His counsel, based on his solid commitment to integrity and to honoring God's Word, has helped me, again and again, to do the right thing, even when it was the hard thing to do.

God intended our lives to be our pulpits. That being the case, Robb Thompson's life loudly speaks of integrity and character. For this reason, I believe he has the moral right to author the book you now hold in your hands.

God's grace has enabled me to author many books of my own, and the forewords to my books have been written by some of the greatest Christian leaders of our generation. I can, however, count on one hand how many times I have felt impressed to write a foreword for someone else. This is one of those times. I count it a great honor that Robb asked me to write the foreword for this book, and I am humbled by the request.

As I read the pages of *The Elephant In The Room: What Many See But Most Ignore*, Robb's words caused me to reflect on my own heart and actions, and I knew I'd want to keep this book nearby for frequent reference. I will reread this book again with my wife at my side, and we will discuss together the truths that call us to change and action. I am sure those truths will have the same transforming effect on you as well.

So before you start reading this book, ask God to open your mind and your heart to truly grasp the truths contained in its pages. Then read and reread these eternal principles, using a pen to underline the words that particularly speak to your heart. And I encourage you — don't walk away from this book until you've read it to the end. Then recommend it to others so they can receive the same benefit.

Rick Renner

Opening Thoughts

The most important structures on earth are not those that grace the beautiful skylines of our great cities. They are not the stunning architectural landmarks applauded and celebrated by historians. Rather, they are the foundations that make it possible for these edifices to stand and endure.

So it is in life. Foundations are vitally important. In fact, while many emphasize the outward accomplishments of their lives, I realize it is the critical, inner structures that we must identify, recognize, and celebrate. The *immovable bedrock* is what I desire to uncover.

I want to know what lies underground, hidden beneath the surface. I want to see what type of foundation a person has, before I hear about the wonderful things he says he can do.

If you are a parent, you are probably well aware of what I am talking about. During your children's formative years, you spend most of your time "underground," working on the foundation of their lives. No one can really see what you're building inside of them during those crucial years, and often, even you don't. But *you* know you're building a foundation of *character.*

As I travel to the nations, it is apparent that the greatest need in our ever-changing global society lies in this arena of character. **Character is**

the foundation upon which all of life is built. Many people spend time building their lives on compromise and mediocrity — only to find out later that such a foundation cannot be sustained.

One good, hard look at the media stories that daily capture our attention is all it takes for us to understand that our society is on a slippery slope of moral decline. Whether it be breaking news stories highlighting corporate greed, the pressures of promiscuity that bombard our teenagers, or a Hollywood icon's fall from grace, we are constantly inundated with examples of poor ethical character.

Declining values in society did not just occur overnight. Poor ethical choices have slowly crept into our society over a long period of time. Like a spider carefully weaving her sticky web in search of prey, immorality has gradually webbed its way throughout every facet of our culture. What's worse, when not confronted, unethical behavior actually becomes a part of our belief system.

Which leads us to **the elephant in the room**. I'm not referring to the flesh-and-blood pachyderm, but to something just as real and just as conspicuous. "The elephant in the room" is a common idiom for an obvious truth that is being avoided. The "elephant" is the glaring reality that everyone sees and is aware of, but is shunned and avoided at all costs.

Isn't that what we have done with ethics in our society? We all know there is a problem with integrity and morality, but it seems as though no one wants to take the lead to confront it. We mistakenly define poor character as something we notice in other people, not necessarily in ourselves. It's easy for us to recognize the wayward politician's lack of judgment...but what about ours? *Do we repeatedly show up late to work? Do we conveniently "forget" to leave a tip at the local cafe? Do we plagiarize information from the Internet, when writing school term papers, and pass it off as our own ideas?* These are uncomfortable questions that need to be addressed. But it's much more comfortable to look the other way, continuing on with our lives as usual.

So here we remain, waiting for someone to take the lead — to confront this beast known as unethical behavior. No longer can we stand around, looking at each other, saying, "You first."..... "No, you!"..... "No, I said YOU!"

Any breakdown in life can invariably be traced back to a breakdown in ethics. That word *ethics* refers to the code of conduct by which we live; the discipline of duty and obligation; the behavior that governs our lives. As we focus on building a foundation of character in our lives, we, of necessity, must build upon the bedrock of ethics and principles. Without a strong, solid foundation of ethical principles undergirding our lives, everything else we attempt to build or accomplish will eventually crumble and fall.

In this book, we are going to explore, in depth, what it takes to be a person of character. But before we do, I urge you to assess where you are, by asking these vital questions:

- *What are the unseen ideals that guide my life?*
- *What are the non-negotiable issues — the principles I will not break?*
- *Am I guided by integrity — or by the convenience of the moment?*

We have the opportunity to shape who we are and to become all that we were created to be. The outcome of our lives rests upon how willingly we embrace truth and virtue — and how strong we build our foundations.

We simply cannot stay the way we are, if we want to achieve great dreams and goals in our lives. We must be willing to change on a daily basis; otherwise, we will become people of *theory* instead of *productivity*.

As we look at the ingredients of strong character, I urge you to be honest with yourself. At first, these truths might be difficult to accept. But here is the good news: No matter how old you are, you can start afresh. Discover, but don't linger upon, the weaknesses in the mortar of your own foundation. Begin to rebuild it into something that is solid and secure. **Make the decision to start pursuing excellent character every single day.** In doing so, you'll find that everything else will fall in line.

Friend, it's time we stood up, looked that elephant straight in the face, and got down to the business of building solid foundations of strong, ethical behavior.

Section 1:

A Fresh Start

A Tower Of Strength

Chapter 1

WE HAD TO HIRE A BIGGER VENUE TO ACCOMMODATE THE ELEPHANT IN THE ROOM

We live in a society where character flaws are frequently ignored — and too often they are even celebrated. Very few people want to face the character problems that have crept into their lives. As a result, they keep building their businesses, careers, marriages, and families on faulty foundations that eventually cause the collapse of everything they have worked all their lives to achieve.

We have an additional problem in Western culture: for years, we have used money to cover up unethical behavior. We have avoided getting honest about our character flaws by continually throwing money at them.

We buy our way out of caring for the elderly by building convalescent centers. We buy our way out of drug addiction by building halfway houses. We buy our way out of parental responsibility by allowing doctors to perform abortions. We buy our youth out of facing consequences by creating overly lenient penalties for their infractions; and the list goes on infinitely.

But we can't indefinitely camouflage our problems and cover our wrongdoings. Money can hide shirked responsibility for only so long. As great a nation as America is, we are living off what our great-great-great-great-grandparents did. We are not getting what *we* deserve at this point in our history; we're receiving the benefits that our *ancestors* deserved. *They paid the price* for good character, sowing seed for a future harvest of prosperity and blessing they would never live to see. And we, the beneficiaries of this abundant harvest, can't expect this prosperity to continue if we persist in encouraging unethical behavior by winking at it.

Unless self-governed by an *internal moral compass*, people will frequently ignore, evade, or directly challenge ethical societal mores. This is the state of affairs in our modern society. We have made poor character acceptable and have become quite adept at taking shortcuts.

For instance, the judicial branch of the U.S. government has been bombarded by an onslaught of precedents, over the past several decades. We are no longer a country that lives with the Constitution of the United States as our guide. We are now a country increasingly governed according to the convictions of morally bankrupt authorities. As a result, certain things are now considered legal in our country that our forefathers would never have tolerated. Some of these laws and practices violate the very principles that produced a people largely known for their strong character. Hence the question: *If the ethical foundations of a nation are destroyed, can it long survive?*

America needs a resurgence of honorable citizens who are committed to pursuing character, integrity, and strong moral dignity. We are the ones who must set that standard for our lives. We must choose to be the kind of people who will not compromise. Each one of us must make the decision to say, "I will always keep my word. If I said I would do it, I will do it."

Now, I understand that there are rare exceptions when a commitment cannot be kept. There are times when the person to whom we gave our word acts dishonorably. I am aware that **a dishonorable person will always require more from us than we have the ability or desire to give.**

But, except in such rare cases, we should determine to keep our word, no matter what. Let's do what we say we are going to do. Let's pay our bills on time and get out of unsecured debt as quickly as possible. Let's ask for forgiveness when we offend someone. Let's care for those who are around us.

You and I must make a choice, today, that we will do what is right in every situation that we face. Sure, we will falter and make mistakes, but let it not be said that we chose to walk unethically or to embrace that which brought harm and destruction to anyone.

What We Really Want

One night, I sat watching a program on the Discovery channel. The program was about a tribe in the deep part of West Africa that had some very unique customs. The men of the tribe had come together to build a hut for one of the men who was getting married. However, there was something unusual about this scenario — the man didn't yet have a bride-to-be! He didn't know who his bride was, but he was building her a hut!

The interpreter asked the man, "Do you know where your wife will come from?"

The man replied, "I had hoped to go to another tribe and bring home a wife. But my father has asked me not to marry outside of ours, for he does not know what foreign customs the woman would bring with her. *I will honor my father's wishes.*"

Then the interpreter asked, "What types of attributes are you looking for, in a woman?"

The man replied, "The number-one attribute I am looking for is *a woman of good character.*"

That primitive West African man had more sense than most people with PhD's!

The book entitled *The Millionaire Mind* includes a survey, in which both middle-class men and millionaires were asked, "What kind of woman

are you looking for, when you marry?" The number-one attribute the middle-class men said they desired was *good looks.* On the other hand, the number-one attribute on the lists of the millionaires was *good character*![1]

I find it very interesting that an American millionaire and a tribal West African man would both come to the same conclusion! Both understood that long after good looks are not so good anymore — long after certain areas of our bodies begin to sag and shape themselves differently — good character remains.

A Solid Foundation

The truth is, many people are looking for others of strong character with whom to associate. In fact, most people make good character a prerequisite for access into their lives, especially when they are scouting for a spouse or looking for a good friend.

But these same people would build better marriages and friendships if they would first examine the character of the person standing in front of the mirror! That assessment would predict the health of their relationships much more accurately than dictating the kind of character they require from others.

Anyone who is searching for a person of excellent character ought to know that such a person is a rare treasure in this world. A faithful person is very difficult to find. It is easier for people to go with the flow than to stand against the tide and do what is right.

I have learned, through the years, that a person who wants to remain irresponsible usually leeches on to individuals who demonstrate responsible, good character. That way, he will always have someone to bear the

load he himself should be carrying. Sad but true, **good character is what others want *you* to possess, so they don't have to.**

There Is Always a Cost!

So, why is a person of character so rare? Because character is expensive. There is a price to pay for pursuing character. It doesn't just happen by chance. We have to passionately, diligently pursue it. **The development of character comes with a price tag; but I can guarantee one thing — it is cheaper than the consequences of living without it!**

It is our family members and close associates who know if we are really men and women of character. They know who we really are. If we have paid the price to pursue character, they, too, have had to endure the pain. They are the ones who have had to go through the hard years with us, when we were being molded through the rejections, the pressures, and the difficulties that built our character.

Others may look at us and say, "I would sure like to have your life!" But how many of those same people would want to pay the price we have had to pay, to get where we are in our pursuit of true character? I have discovered that **life doesn't give us what we want or what we think we should have. Life gives us what we work for — what we deserve!**

Nevertheless, the prize is always greater than the price. Nothing good can ever be built in our lives without good character. It affects every area of our personal existence — our decisions, our words, our actions, our attitudes, our goals, and our relationships.

Root Failures

If we do not fix our character before we attempt to work on anything else in life, we will only experience failure after failure. We may begin to build, but it will crumble. We may attempt to prosper, but it will be as if our purses have large holes in them. We may expend enormous amounts of energy, but all our efforts will come to nothing.

How do we avoid that oh-so-dangerous pitfall in life? First, we must realize that **we may not always be rewarded for our strong traits, but we will most definitely be disqualified for the weak ones!**

As it has been commonly said, a chain is only as strong as its weakest link. It might be a huge, 1,000-link chain with 999 super-strong links and only one weak link. The integrity of that chain will not depend on its 999 strong links but, rather, the single weak one.

Just consider what might happen if that huge chain is used in an international tractor-pull competition by the reigning ten-year champion. Suppose this champion decides he does not need to check the integrity of the chain, because it appears to be so hefty and strong.

As the tractor pull begins, the champion is confident, since he has such a huge chain to rely on. He pulls with all his might, waving smugly at the crowd, as his tractor moves past his opponents. But as he continues to put pressure on the chain, the one weak link suddenly breaks, and that huge chain snaps in half!

Meanwhile, his competitors just chug along, a few inches at a time. Their chains don't look as huge, but they have integrity. Little by little, they inch forward to the finish line.

Here is the simple lesson: **Build character with no known weaknesses,**

point yourself in the right direction, then move slowly and deliberately, determining never to stop until you have reached your desired destination.

That's why it must be our constant desire to focus on constructing the foundation of character. Everything in life rests squarely upon that bedrock.

Every failure — whether in marriage, in one's personal habits, in the workplace, in business, or in public policy — can be traced back to a failure in character, almost 100 percent of the time.

The Predictor of Success

If we want to understand how to achieve *lasting* success, we must realize that sustained favor and increase are directly linked to the kind of character we demonstrate, as we walk through life. The personal, professional, and relational advancements we may periodically experience will be empty and fleeting if we continue to betray our conscience and walk in compromise. Success can only happen to the extent that we are willing to plant the fertile seeds of character. In other words, we cannot enjoy a lasting harvest unless our lives are firmly rooted and entrenched in these ever-so-important traits. **Lasting success is inseparably joined to the portrait painted by the brush of our character.**

So many people suffer the heartache of having their lives and relationships uprooted and torn away from success and happiness. Many spend decades striving to reach their goals, without ever seeing them come to pass. To believe in the truth of a principle is not enough. If character hasn't been rooted deeply within a man's heart — the place where dreams originate — he may stand for a little while, but eventually his hopes will be shattered on the rocks of time.

Character has the ability to firmly hold on to principle, without letting go. It causes a man to relentlessly cling to integrity and truth. **Character provides the essential ingredients for *accomplished* goals and *realized* dreams.**

Many men and women live their lives by emotion rather than by principle. Emotions never provide a basis for good decision-making. In fact, it is, at times, dangerous to be driven by them. Granted, by emotionally expressing negative feelings, people take pressure off themselves, at least in the short term. But unless the root cause of their problem is dealt with, the pressure is sure to return.

People who live by their emotions often want to know what good things are going to happen to them in the future. It is important to understand that no good can come of our future if we refuse to take care of the character flaws that live in the present.

There will be no bright future for us if we refuse to confront the weaknesses in our character; for as soon as we arrive at tomorrow, it will become "today" — complete with the same problems that are keeping us in our present limitations.

In Hot Pursuit

So, we must determine to fix where we are right now, remembering to remain more interested in improving *our own* character than in judging the lack of it in others. Before we can be promoted to the next level, we will need to ask the appropriate questions and discover what must be corrected in our human experience.

We must never ask questions about tomorrow, if we are not challenging the standards by which we live today. First, we must discover what is hindering our *present* progress; then, we must take the necessary steps to deal with those weaknesses. As we do, the questions of tomorrow will take care of themselves.

As a person who wants to excel in character, make every effort to discover the changes you need to make in your most important relationships:

- *Find out what your employer would have you do to become more valuable to him.*
- *Ask your spouse how you can better fulfill your role as a wife or a husband.*
- *If you are a son or a daughter, go to your parents and find out how you can become more pleasing to them.*

Make it your aim to display character in a greater way, every day of your life.

What are some of the factors that help us strengthen our character? Instruction should be at the top of our list; but, more often than not, hardship is. **If we will not learn when someone instructs us, we will be forced to learn when consequences come to teach us.**

Interestingly, if we respond to problems and trials with a positive, consistent attitude, they will be good for us — they will help us learn to endure. Endurance will develop strength of character in us, and that character will strengthen our confident expectation of success.

What Is This Thing Called Character?

Character is the sum total of the inner principles by which we live our lives. It is the mental and moral features, whether good or evil, that define us, as individuals.

Good character refers to the virtue, self-discipline, and honorable constitution an individual possesses. It also means moral strength. When a person possesses this quality, he refuses to be moved away from principle, no matter what anyone says or does. In fact, **a person of strong character esteems moral strength of greater value than beauty, riches, or fame.**

The words character and integrity are intimately connected. The root word for "integrity" is *tom* or *tome*, from the root word *tamam*. It means *completeness, prosperity, innocence, fullness,* or *uprightness at a venture.* It also carries the meaning of *being whole, upright, made perfect and entire, lacking nothing.* The dictionary tells us that integrity refers to *moral soundness or purity, uprightness of character,* and *honesty.*

Integrity is the uncompromising desire to do what is right, in every situation, regardless of the circumstances. It implies an inflexible adherence to the highest standard of values and behavior. Integrity transcends age, race, religion, education, gender, and personality.

Integrity can also be defined as a person's inward attributes, motives, and qualities of virtue, that outwardly manifest as one's moral and ethical standard. Integrity is uprightness and purity in the very essence of a person. It speaks of a pure, untouched singleness of heart, with no pretense or duplicity.

Character is the foundation. Character demonstrates integrity throughout the challenging situations of life. Without it, we will never succeed in our other pursuits, for that foundation applies to *every* other realm we will ever enter.

- In marriage, character is gentleness.
- In the home, it is respect.
- In business, it is integrity.
- In society, it is courtesy.
- In the workplace, it is diligence.
- In sports, it is fairness.
- In relationship, it is kindness.
- Toward the victors in life, character is congratulations.
- Toward the victims, it is protection.
- Toward wrongdoers, it is resistance.
- Toward the less fortunate, it is a hand up.
- Toward the strong, it is trust.
- Toward the contrite, it is restoration.
- And toward yourself, it is the willingness to hear the truth and to change.

So determine to be *all* that you can be. Pursue excellence in character with all your heart, soul, mind, and strength. Start building an enduring foundation that will uphold the highest and best, in every area of your life!

"STANDARDS HAVEN'T FALLEN. EXCELLENCE BECAME CONSIDERED TOO FUSSY."

Honor Bound

Chapter 2

"HAVE YOU NOTICED IT, TOO?"

I am interested in the way you and I walk this journey called life. I have an insatiable desire for people of deep ethics and character to be known as the most valuable that anyone could ever find to work with, rely on, and relate to, on an everyday basis. But to achieve that goal, we must become both honorable and indispensable to those around us, not only in the workplace but also in our homes, our places of worship, our communities, our relationships, and in every other arena of life.

How do we become indispensable people of honor? First, we must *focus on eliminating the unprofitable hindrances of our past.* Then, we must *begin to build into our lives certain key ingredients that are both profitable and essential to people of strong character.*

With this in mind, I want to share some keys that will help us in our quest to become invaluable to the people around us. These guidelines will change our lives if we will take them seriously and act upon them, as opportunities arise.

Time to Clean Ship

1. Disconnect from unprofitable relationships.

It is essential that we free ourselves from dishonorable relationships that threaten our commitment to good character. If those relationships haven't bitten us yet, they most assuredly will if we are not vigilant! We have to separate ourselves now, so that when the time comes for the

hammer of consequence to fall on their lives, we will be far away, enjoying the benefits of our commitment to moral integrity.

2. Eliminate unprofitable attitudes.

We must live our lives without criticizing, judging, or whining, actively steering clear of pessimistic, questioning cynics and those who stir up attitudes of dishonor, dissatisfaction, sarcasm, and doubt within us.

Most people whom we meet along the road of life are usually doing one of four things: *murmuring, complaining, faultfinding, or grumbling.*

They may start by murmuring under their breath. If you ask them if anything is wrong, they'll say, "No, nothing is really wrong." But if you ask if anything is *right*, in their lives, they will make it obvious that nothing is really right, either! They just keep murmuring until, finally, their murmuring becomes more vocal, and they start voicing their complaints.

For instance, they may say, "I've been trying this 'ethical character' stuff for a while now, and I'll tell you what — life was better when I was lying and cheating and partying! At least back then, I could think whatever I wanted to think and say whatever I wanted to say; people weren't always nagging me about my attitudes and words. They weren't continually talking to me about straightening out my life. I just want to be able to do what I want to do, without caring about what anyone else thinks about it!"

On and on these attitudes grow, becoming more and more negative by the minute. After a long bout of complaining, people often start finding fault with others, in order to take the pressure off themselves. This critical attitude becomes extremely contagious, prompting others to murmur and complain, as well.

Another reason people grumble and find fault with others is that they

are discouraged about themselves. Because they don't have anything positive going on, **the only way they can feel better about themselves is by tearing someone else down to their level of immaturity.**

People don't find fault with others unless they have faults of their own that they don't want to deal with. A person is in danger of being judged, himself, when he judges and finds fault with others. Why is this true? Because, usually, he is practicing the very same trespasses that he is judging others over! Whenever he criticizes or dishonors others, he actually makes himself guilty, without excuse.

Jesus wisely said that people need to get the two-by-four beam out of their own eye, before they ever pick up a magnifying glass and a pair of tweezers in an attempt to surgically remove the tiny particle of sawdust from their brother's eye!

The message appears clear: We are to work on eliminating *our own* wrong attitudes, while allowing others to take care of themselves!

Building Blocks

1. *Build into your life integrity, honesty, and a sense of honor.*

Great reward awaits the man or woman who will invest the time, attention, and energy required to build a strong foundation of character. Character will blossom only as we run *toward* the challenges and trials of life, not away from them. As we respond to each test with a winning, "can-do" attitude, we will discover that those tests are just opportunities in disguise! Although pain is the instrument that carves us into individuals of character, that pain and that character often become our platform for promotion.

2. *Build into your life profitable relationships that will challenge and provoke your character to higher standards.*

Wisdom advises us to search for honorable individuals, whose excellence in character far exceeds our own. How? First, *we identify our strongest character traits.* Then, *we find someone who would consider that level of character to be a weakness within his own character profile.* That is the person we should pursue and emulate!

We have already talked quite a bit about honesty and integrity. However, I want to take the subject a little further in this context of becoming indispensable to others.

We would probably all agree that the one thing we would love to have in our lives is more honest people — people who actually *are* who they claim to be — so we could believe what they say. As I'm sure you are well aware, many individuals *claim* to be loyal and trustworthy — but finding such a person can be nearly impossible! The attribute of integrity is a priceless commodity in our world.

The person of integrity is an honorable individual. When he says something, it's as good as gold, as far as everyone else is concerned. There is no mixture in what he says — only a pure, undefiled wholeness. And because he is a person of honor, he will not take advantage of a situation for his own benefit. He knows that there is much more to life than what he can accumulate for himself.

3. *Make the choices that lead toward your purpose and assignment in life.*

We have the ability to choose the direction we go in all areas of life. We also have the responsibility to choose *the honorable way* in every decision we make.

Let's take the selection of a job, as an example. We need to allow the wisdom of proven principles to lead us to the job that is right for us at the present time.

Most people have a problem with the job they currently have. They wish they had a different one. They are constantly thinking, "I wish I was doing something else — a job that I like."

But often, the problem isn't the job. It is a mind-set of discontent that is ubiquitous in today's society. People who feel this way might very likely feel the same way in a different job position.

If we find ourselves continually complaining about our present job, perhaps we need to consider finding something else. We will need to stay alert, for we may have only a short window of opportunity to find out how to get where we need to go.

After we find a new position by filtering all prospects through the "principle filter," we must then *choose to succeed* at that job. In fact, we must be determined to succeed in every area of life, for **success is an inner decision long before it becomes apparent in our outward circumstances.**

"But I don't know if I can do it."

You *can* do it! There is nothing that is too great for you to do. If we choose to walk honorably in all that we do, then honor's answer to us is "*yes.*" It isn't "no" or "maybe." Honor doesn't say, "Well, I don't know if *you* can. Maybe someone else can, but you can't."

Everything we put our hands to *can* succeed. Our job *can* prosper. When we choose to live our lives in moral integrity and ethical character, our place of business will prosper *just because we are there* — just because we showed up on the scene! The people with whom we do business

will get more business, just because they're doing business with us. People will benefit just by associating with us. And in every situation, *we win!*

Crown of Honor

There must be a sense of honor that accompanies us wherever we go. Honor must cover all our dealings with other people and define the way we carry ourselves in every situation. If anyone is ever going to be upset with us, let it be over our honesty and our firm stance, when it comes to honor. No longer can we upset others by "taking them to the cleaners" again, after they decided to trust us one more time. **Character carries itself with honor through every situation of life.**

It is imperative that we are honorable in all that we do. We must never break the principle of honor. As we live in this manner, people will begin to recognize us as individuals who aren't seeking our own benefit but, instead, upholding high ethics in every situation. They will see that doing the honorable thing means more to us than personal gain.

Let's talk about being a person of honor in the workplace for a moment. As employees, we need to be pleasing and compliant to our superiors. Our service to them needs to come from the sincere motive of our heart — not merely an outward compliance that hides an inward grumbling.

Of course, if a superior tells us to do something unethical, we have to say, "With great respect, I have to say no. I can't do that." However, if we have already been living our lives honorably before that superior, he will understand our response. More than likely, he would not even ask us to do something that is out of character for us.

On the other hand, if we have *not* been living our lives honorably before our employer, we shouldn't expect much sympathy when we say, "I can't do that. That would be stealing." He is likely to reply, "Well, why can't you? You did it yesterday."

"What do you mean?"

"You had someone else punch in for you at eight o'clock, and you didn't show up until almost nine."

Or maybe he would say, "You spent twenty-five minutes on your fifteen-minute break."

Or perhaps this one hits closer to home: "Yesterday you spent most of your time on the phone, making personal phone calls, and on the Internet, visiting Facebook and Twitter."

You may say, "Oh, but my boss doesn't mind if I come in a little late or talk on the phone during work hours."

Please let me help you — *there is no such thing as an employer who doesn't mind.* There may be a boss who doesn't say anything, but every boss cares about how honorably his employees conduct themselves in the workplace.

Here is something to consider: **Integrity will not always be rewarded BY this life, but integrity will always be rewarded IN this life.** This is a truth we really need to think about. When we walk in honor, we will be given honor. As we live honorably in our place of business and elsewhere, we will find that we are highly sought-after, simply because honor is such a rare quality. However, we shouldn't expect everyone we meet to be happy with us. Some people will actually turn on us because of our integrity.

That's all right. Regardless of what other people do, our goal must always be to demonstrate honor. We are not honorable because we think it will

do anything for us. We are honorable because we live our lives by principle.

In the coming days, this is the only way we will be able to live if we want to be successful. Until now, many individuals have appeared to profit from playing ethical games. Perhaps we have gotten away with fudging on principles in the past. But now is the time to eliminate the sloppy lifestyle we have previously allowed. It is time for us to pursue a virtuous lifestyle.

Go the Extra Mile

Another choice we must make is to "go the extra mile." If someone asks us to go *one* mile in our duties and assignments, we should make the honorable choice to go *two*. Honor always goes above and beyond its duty — *it under-promises and over-performs.* **"Extra-Mile Road" is the boulevard of choice for a person of character.**

I have, however, noticed something, over the years, about this principle of going the extra mile. Sometimes, when people begin to understand this principle, they eagerly start doing extra things at their job, in their home, etc. The problem is, they get so distracted by "going the extra mile" that they never finish what they were instructed to do in the first place!

To avoid imbalance, we should refrain from "going the extra mile" until we have completed our prior responsibilities. That is how we make sure that we stay valuable to our superiors. We can make the effort to do our primary job faster and more efficiently than usual. That way, we can do some *extra* things for our superiors in the same amount of time that it takes others to finish their normal responsibilities.

Remember, our superiors are looking for problem-solvers. They ask questions such as: *"What kind of problems does this individual solve? What kind of assets does he bring to the table? Is this person's presence a benefit, or is it more of a hassle?"*

We need to know how to go beyond being hard workers. We should get to a place where we're not only doing what we are paid to do, but we are also finding ways to put icing on our superior's cake for him. That is how we can become extremely valuable to those around us — not only in the workplace but everywhere!

One more thing about becoming indispensable in the workplace: An honorable employee never picks up a poor attitude about his or her wages. If we want to negotiate with our superior about a raise in pay, that is what we need to do. Meanwhile, we must fulfill, with excellence, the agreement we originally made. We must keep our word. It is imperative that we do so.

"Well, yes, but those other employees make more than I do, and they have the same job!"

Now, wait a minute. That is one of those areas that is not our responsibility; therefore, we shouldn't even have an opinion about it.

I'm all for people making good wages. None of us need to sit around and think, "He makes too much money. I don't think he's worth it." We are free to just say, "I'm going to excel over little, and then I will be put in charge over more. I am *not* going to move off ethical principles, just so I can make more money. As an honorable individual, I value principle far more than ill-gained prosperity!"

All these keys are important, as we face the challenges of today's modern age. They make us valuable to the people we work with, live with,

and interact with, on a daily basis. And in the workplace, these keys can make us indispensable to those companies that are, right now, undergoing tremendous internal changes.

In the workplace, at home, in our places of worship, in our relationships — wherever we are, we should focus on bringing great value to the table, as people of honor and integrity. Let's choose to be problem-solvers who always go the extra mile to serve and, thus, make ourselves indispensable!

DANAE... YOU CAN'T EXPECT TO ALTER REALITY JUST BY SAYING IT OFFENDS YOU
WHOA, POTTY-MOUTH! MY CULTURE FORBIDS ANY USE OF THE "R" WORD!!
THAT'S ANOTHER THING... YOU CAN'T JUST MAKE UP YOUR OWN RULES AND DEMAND EVERYONE RESPECT IT AS A CULTURE
OH... REALLY?
THEN HOW DID ALL THE OTHER CULTURES GET STARTED?
WAIT... YOU'RE STARTING WHAT?
A NEW CULTURE... ONE WITHOUT CHILDREN
©'09 WILEY INK, INC. 12-18
DIST. BY UNIVERSAL UCLICK WILEYINK@EARTHLINK.NET GOCOMICS.COM/NONSEQUITUR

Set In Your Ways

Chapter 3

ONLY ALAN WAS PREPARED TO ACKNOWLEDGE THE ELEPHANT IN THE ROOM.
harrop
www.cartoonstock.com

So where do we start in our search for the ingredients of good and honorable character? How do we discover the character traits we are to develop in our lives?

A person of character lives by a code of strict personal ethics. He has identified the answers to some of life's crucial questions, such as: *What are my absolutes? What do I consider to be the non-negotiables in my life?* Only when we identify and begin to honor the *absolutes* in our lives, will our future be productive.

After making the commitment to live our lives in this manner, we will likely come to realize that many individuals trust an honorable man's character more than they trust their own! They know they can trust the word of a person with strong character. They know he will live by his principles, no matter what the cost.

We must choose to walk as honorable men and women who will keep our word, knowing it may cost us all we are or have, and trusting that true prosperity will follow principle in every situation.

Another non-negotiable in the lives of virtuous people is their commitment to excellence in all that they do. They understand that **today's excellence is tomorrow's mediocrity.** So, they continually search for ways to improve, and they welcome opportunities to be corrected and instructed.

Receiving correction cheerfully is a prerequisite for character development. We tend to believe that we can live our lives without allowing others to correct us. It is not until we realize our natural tendency

toward mediocrity — and just how prone we are to self-centeredness or lying to ourselves — that we recognize our utter need for the corrective guidance of a moral compass. We realize that, in reality, we can do nothing without an immovable ethical standard.

We will continue to lose the race, in our own lives, as long as we seek to be rewarded for our good points, while refusing to recognize our weaknesses. **We can never change what we are unwilling to face.**

People who refuse to recognize their weak points seldom take responsibility for their mistakes and failures. Instead, they look to blame others for the pain they have created for themselves.

If we need help in getting over a weakness, we should not be afraid to go to someone we can trust. Only when we admit our need for help, will help arrive. However, we must first be willing to change. We cannot just dismiss the issue by saying, "Well, I guess I made a mistake." Until we recognize, confront, and *conquer* our weaknesses, we will just keep wondering why we are not celebrated.

Principled Living

Character does what is right, even in the face of possible rejection. Answering to our own conscience, we must be faithful to principle, without fail. Even if a person acts unfaithfully toward us, he will still be the beneficiary of our commitment to integrity. **If we live by principle, we must never allow ourselves to be affected by the moods and emotions of others.**

A person who has neglected to establish clear non-negotiables or to elevate his "personal integrity quotient" cannot predict how he will act in any given situation. He basically waits until he is in the middle of a

challenge to decide how he "feels" like responding. He is like a ship adrift, with no headings and void of destination.

Let's choose, instead, to have an inner motivation for personal growth, and then translate that motivation into "motivaction"! Passionate pursuit guarantees that we will be found worthy of promotion and greater responsibility. It will connect us with dynamic people — people of character who live their lives on a higher plane and who can promote us to a higher place as well.

Other people are to be the beneficiaries of our commitment to unbending principle. Life is simple when we understand this precept — not easy, but simple. We no longer have to deal with people on the basis of *their* words or actions. Instead, we deal with them according to *our* inner ideals and value system!

When we choose a character-driven life, we possess the ability to display the following qualities in relationship:

- **Love** — The way we love others reflects our commitment to compassion and truth.
- **Integrity** — The way we treat others reveals the strength or weakness of our own character.
- **Respect** — The way we respect others is the way we respect ourselves. Disrespect for others reveals that we have not yet learned to respect ourselves.
- **Honesty and Virtue** — The way we keep our word to others is the way we keep our word to our own conscience and code of honor. If one doesn't keep his word to others, he has not yet kept his word to himself.

- **Generosity** — The way we invest in others reveals what we believe about our own future. If we believe our lives have purpose, we will *purposefully give.*
- **Loyalty** — If we are disloyal to others, we are unfaithful to the potential and promise within ourselves.
- **Compliance and Submission** — If we don't submit ourselves to the appointed authorities in our lives, we haven't submitted ourselves to the protection of wisdom and instruction.

For the sake and benefit of others, we must, first and foremost, desire to walk in love. We must always remember that love is undeniably *linked to our actions, not just our emotions.* Love isn't just a collection of words or feelings. Love has to do with our attitudes, our posture, and our approach toward other people. It has to do with demonstrating a true servant's heart and valuing others as we desire to be valued.

We may have regrets concerning our lack of character in the past — but what good is it to keep on worrying about it? There is nothing we can do about yesterday. However, if we will change *today*, tomorrow will be different.

Those of character always choose to live life by the highest standards. It is time that we get back to our foundations and begin to once more embrace non-negotiable *standards* of moral fortitude! It's time to search out what character and integrity really mean and embrace the character traits by which we are to live our lives.

STANDARDS

The classical application of the word *standard* refers to a flag, a banner, or a sign used as a rallying point around which the troops gathered and from which they attacked an enemy. The word *standard* refers to an established and recognized criterion of excellence; a beginning point; a bottom line; a foundational principle or value *from which a person refuses to retreat.*

When we choose to embrace *high standards* in our lives, as "a flag or a banner," those standards become a rallying point *around which* we can gather for protection from unhealthy decisions and unwelcome consequences in our lives. They are also a rallying point *from which* we can effectively attack and defeat personal complacency, mediocrity, and barrenness.

These values and standards become our established criterion of excellence and integrity. When the insipid, mediocre tendencies of daily living threaten to steal our dreams and undermine our goals, those *higher standards* become a lifeline. Our dreams are preserved, and the impact of our lives is optimized, as we raise our standard to a higher level of integrity, purity, honor, respect, commitment, obedience, service, and excellence. This higher standard then becomes our new bottom line, from which we are never to withdraw.

Each of us must make a choice. If we say no to this higher standard, we opt out of the dynamic future that was meant to be ours. But if we say yes, we immediately tap into greater *protection* and *power to discern wisdom,* thereby enhancing our ability to springboard into unparalleled achievement.

Here are some simple steps to honorable and effective living:

1. ***Never compromise a standard to which you've already committed.***
2. ***Protect and maintain established standards.***
3. ***Embrace ever-higher standards, as you eagerly pursue change, maturity, and growth in character.***

We are all in this race, and each of us should be pressing toward the finish line that lies before us. After all, **the only meaningful goal of life is to become all that we were created to be.**

Character qualities of love, loyalty, integrity, honor, service, and compliance create the blueprint that leads us to excellence of character in our lives. However, it is up to us to make that blueprint come alive, as we work on constructing a solid *foundation* of character — little by little, brick by brick — in preparation for undergirding the dreams we are called to fulfill in this life.

UH-OH...
THERE ARE NO ABSOLUTES IN LIFE
...LOOKS LIKE A JOB FOR...
OBVIOUSMAN
DUH
HOLD IT RIGHT THERE, YOU SEMANTIC NE'ER-DO-WELL...
YOUR SIGN MAKES AN **ABSOLUTE** STATEMENT, THUS CONTRADICTING YOUR SO-CALLED BELIEFS!
THERE ARE NO ABSOLUTES IN LIFE
?
WILEY
THERE ARE NO ABSOLUTES IN LIFE
WELL... YES... BUT NO... I MEAN...
...OK ...UH... LITERALLY... BUT IN THE FIGURATIVE
URK
FOOM
THANK YOU, OBVIOUSMAN!!
NO TIME FOR ANY GLORY-BASKING, FOLKS.
THE PRESIDENTIAL CANDIDATES ARE HEADING THIS WAY...
11-7 ©1999 Wiley Miller / Dist. by Washington Post Writers Group
E-mail: wiley@wileytoons.com See HOMER on the web: www.wileytoons.com

Facing Your Giants

Chapter 4

"WE DON'T MENTION THE ROOM IN THE ELEPHANT"

As we build our lives upon the solid bedrock of character, we must remember one key: **Unless we learn to focus on our future, we will be continually limited by the nightmares of our past.** At this point, each of us can probably recognize traits within our own character that, if ignored, could threaten our dreams for future success. *What steps must be taken to free ourselves from the mistakes of the past, in order to embrace character and wise decision-making in the future?*

As our hunger for change grows, we quickly discover that we have to deal with *ourselves* every day! We begin to ask, *"Why am I the way I am? Why do I sometimes sabotage my own efforts, when I know I have treasure within me that can change the world?"*

When these questions start to arise, we must attempt to find out who has been talking to us every day, through all those years of disappointment and defeat. What are the things that have determined our lives and made us the way we are? And how can we begin to change into the men and women we must be?

To begin with, we have to understand some facts about our lives on this earth. Every human being is born with certain "determinisms." These are factors that, unless withstood, will determine the outcome of a person's life. In fact, the term "determinism" implies the concept of "that from which there is no escape." There are three types of determinisms that influence the nature of every individual: *Genetic Determinisms, Psychological Determinisms,* and *Environmental Determinisms.*

These three forces are constantly at work in our lives, molding our characters, personalities, and futures. Barring a quality decision to aggressively resist the inevitability of these forces, these three factors will determine who we become in life.

Genetic Determinisms

First, let's talk about genetic determinisms. All our physical attributes (whether brown eyes or blue eyes, short or tall, thick or thin) were given to us by the genetics of our parents, our grandparents, our great-grandparents, and our great-great-grandparents. All these people in our family lines have helped make us who we are.

But much more than physical attributes can be passed down from generation to generation. On the negative side, susceptibility to certain vices or a tendency to contract certain diseases can also be passed down.

The medical community acknowledges that people are "predisposed" to certain ailments and diseases. For instance, let's look at the problem of alcoholism. A child who has alcoholic parents will quite often deal with the same issue in his own life. The same is true for heart disease, high blood pressure, mental illness, and so forth.

We may not necessarily see every generation dealing with these genetic predispositions. They may skip a generation; or an individual may develop a resistance to a particular habit or vice — but then, one generation later, it will show up strong.

Each of our lives is actually a culmination of approximately four hundred years of family history. The shortcomings and weaknesses of the fathers are passed down into the third and fourth generations. That means every fault, every problem, and every propensity toward wrong,

with which our ancestors struggled, has been passed down from generation to generation; and, over the years, we have had to deal with these issues in our own lives. To say it another way, the temptations and inappropriate desires that periodically challenge each of us are a manifestation of four generations of struggle. They are all a part of our genetic determinisms.

Our forefathers may or may not have been able to overcome the vices, habits, or diseases that troubled them. Nevertheless, defeat does not have to be *our* portion. We have a choice to make — a choice that is absolutely essential if we are ever going to live as people of character.

If we will choose right character, we will destroy the giant named yesterday. It is of the utmost importance that we break the power of our past. We must decide to go beyond our hereditary limitations and do more than those who have come before us. We can determine, *by choice*, to be different!

It is up to us to make sure that we break the back of our genetic determinisms. We must destroy the bad habits and destructive appetites that were passed down to us through our genes, so we can be free to live productive and fulfilling lives.

Psychological Determinisms

Secondly, we must deal with our psychological determinisms. Stated simply, *what we think* is who we are and who we will become. Some may say, "I don't believe that!" But that doesn't change the facts.

This concept of psychological determinisms is the very thing that slammed me around and mentally beat me up, until that day, in 1975,

when, in a mental institution, I had a life-changing breakthrough. I began to learn how to keep my mind, will, and emotions healthy, by utilizing this principle: *As I think in my heart, so am I.*

To determine your own psychological determinisms, consider these questions:

- *What do you allow your mind to dwell on?*
- *What do you let yourself listen to?*
- *What are the things that most influence your life?*
- *Who is the person who has most influenced your life?*

Many times, when people try to think of the individual who has most influenced their lives, they say, "Oh, that would be my mom. She has influenced me so much." Or they reply, "The person who most influenced me was my wonderful teacher in the third grade."

No, the people who have influenced us the most just so happen to be those who are controlling our minds, right this second, with the hurts, disappointments, or offenses they have caused us. That is what we are dwelling on. Those are the issues we have been mulling over and over in our minds, while doing what we can to live productive lives. These voices from the past have become our primary psychological determinisms.

Once again, our thinking habits determine our performance. **We will never perform in a manner that is inconsistent with the way we see ourselves.**

Environmental Determinisms

Thirdly, our environmental determinisms include where we live, what kind of culture and values we are exposed to, and the circumstances that surround us throughout our lives.

Do you realize that, in this world today, there are people who live and die within a one-mile radius? They think they have everything they need inside that one mile, so that's as far as they ever go.

As I was growing up, my mom didn't want me to go past a certain street in my neighborhood. But I can remember always longing to venture outside of that boundary—always looking for an escape from the less-than-perfect environment I was living in. Somehow, I realized that **in order to achieve success in the future, one must break the glass ceilings of the past.**

Many people spend their whole lives looking for greener grass on the other side, all the while bemoaning their present circumstances. They become "excusiologists," attempting to use their genetic, psychological, and environmental backgrounds as their excuse for not achieving success in life. For instance, they might say:

- *"I had a difficult childhood."*
- *"I'm not of the favored race."*
- *"I've never had enough money."*
- *"I was born on the wrong side of the tracks."*

This list of excuses is inexhaustible, but every excuse reflects the attitude of the excusiologist: "All these predetermined conditions are just wrong, wrong, wrong, wrong, wrong! If only *they* were different, everything would be different for me."

But it doesn't really matter where we came from or what color we are. There are advantages and disadvantages to *every* genetic and environmental background. We just need to become sensitive to understanding and acknowledging our *advantages*. Then, as we are diligent to walk as people of character, we will be prepared to walk through the doors of opportunity that life opens for us.

Destined by Choice

Our *personal choices* will determine either our final escape from or our continued slavery to these predetermined forces that tend to govern our lives from the moment of birth.

Out of the very few people who are willing to embrace change, most fall into two distinct categories. *First, there are those who are willing to forsake an old pattern but never embrace the new.* They make a valiant effort to break free from their negative determinisms; however, they do not use that freedom to build a new life or bring freedom to others.

Secondly, there are those who attempt to embrace new habits but never disown the old. They get very enthusiastic and excited when they hear about new ways of success. They are learners, always aspiring for more, yet unwilling to let go of what is familiar and comfortable. They do not realize that these new truths cannot work in conjunction with the old mindsets and vices.

It's quite interesting that our modern society now calls many of these vices *diseases* or *alternative lifestyles.* For instance, alcoholism is now labeled a disease. Even people who otherwise live morally sometimes use that definition to justify their drinking habits. As long as these individuals can get enough people to agree that their actions are excusable and acceptable, they will continue to live in deception. Friend, we must **never attempt to give life to something that should be put to death.**

What is a person to do if he wants to get rid of that "gene" of alcoholism? Wisdom provides the answer: *He is to be filled with something greater and more satisfying.* Rather than merely attempting to eradicate the bad, he must *replace* the bad with a *greater good.* When a person purposes to do things this way, no habit is unbreakable!

So many people still struggle with yesterday — with flaws and habits that have held them captive for so many years. Many work very hard to justify and convince themselves (and others) that they are winning; however, deep down inside, they are unwilling to forsake the familiar and abandon themselves to change.

But a person of character refuses to cling to the comfort and mediocrity of his past. Instead, he lives his life by the following truth: **There is no future in the past.**

If we are going to walk in newness of character, we must hold fast to the truth about who we are. We must not allow the past to dictate the future. No matter what we, or others, may be seeing at the moment, we must each believe that our old, lazy self can be transformed, as we *choose* the way of character.

We must listen only to what integrity has to say, for that is the genuine truth concerning who we really are. Our poor selves, our confused selves, and our old depressed selves will become a thing of the past, as we embrace principle-driven lives!

"But you just don't know the pressure I'm under and the temptations I face. It's too much to bear sometimes!"

It is inspiring to hear what wealthy tycoon and philanthropist, W. Clement Stone, once said, when one of his fourteen secretaries approached him, fretting, "Mr. Stone, we have a big problem on the East Coast."

Stone replied, "Wonderful. Problems make me strong. Give it to me."

Now, there's an attitude all of us should adopt in life! Most of us spend our lives either running from problems we see in ourselves or denying that they even exist. We must remember that the initial step to all change is admitting that we have a problem. Then we must pursue

wisdom, in order to solve the problem. Nothing but wisdom and truth will give us the answers we need to walk in victory and joy in this life.

Each of us will experience tremendous growth if we will simply start each and every day by telling ourselves, *"I am dead to the challenges of my past, but I am alive to a promising, productive, and purposeful future. Therefore, I will not give my mind or my body to that which would cause me to go backward. I will only give my mind and body to the things that add value to my life!"* As we confidently speak these words aloud, so our own ears can hear them, our perspective will begin to change.

This is the first step toward facing our giants and walking in the advantages of ethics and character. This is also the answer to the question, *"Why do so many people experience defeat and a breakdown of character in their lives?"* People suffer a breakdown in character when they continue to allow yesterday to control them and to dictate their direction in life.

That *never* has to describe us, friend! We no longer have to remain under the crippling circumstances of our past. We can choose, on purpose, to live by a new set of rules. But we must put this truth to work in our lives on a regular basis, by giving ourselves a daily dose of affirmation and encouragement!

Positive self-talk will affirm who we are and where we are going. As we speak these truths aloud, boldly and often, *until the truth of our words sinks deep down into our hearts,* we will find that, whenever problems and temptations arise throughout the day, it will be much easier to act according to the new people we have *chosen* to be, not according to the dead-end determinisms of our past.

Once we have made these truths alive and active in our hearts, we will have taken the first step toward becoming individuals of ethics and character. We will know that every time we choose to do what is right, no matter what the cost, we will only be acting according to who we really are!

You Reap What You Sow

Chapter 5

"I'm right there in the room, and no one even acknowledges me."

To excel in character, we must come to the place where we recognize the necessity for *absolutes* in our lives. That means every personal action and choice is determined by a pre-set code of principles, which becomes our decision-maker, even when the world thrusts its pain upon us.

As we embrace right principles, even in the face of great opposition, the tide will begin to turn for us, and success will begin flowing in our direction.

This is not an overnight process. It takes time to learn how to walk this out. **The summation of the principles by which we daily live our lives** *(the extent to which we act on what is right, even when it hurts)* **will determine how much favor and real success we walk in.**

Must Be Tested

Strong character is tested character. Abraham Lincoln is a good example of a man who walked in character and integrity, no matter what anyone else said or did. But "Honest Abe" didn't learn how to walk as a man of principle overnight. He endured many difficult challenges through the years, as the trials of life tested his character. He is remembered as one of the United States of America's most beloved presidents; yet, he endured failure after failure in his personal life and political career. History records that Mr. Lincoln lost eighteen elections

and suffered several heartbreaking personal setbacks before he was elected to be president.

Until the time came for his influence to come to the forefront, Mr. Lincoln's character was tested in private, each test revealing whether or not he would consistently do the right thing. Through each challenge, he passed the test, and the day came when he was promoted to lead America through what could possibly be called her most embarrassing hour — the Civil War.

Whether we realize it or not, we are being tested at this very moment. *Will we do what is right, or will we compromise? Will we do what is convenient and easy, or what is difficult but ethical?*

Each and every trial we face drives us either closer to or further away from our purpose in life. We will eventually reap the consequences of every choice we make. Every time we make a choice, we sow a seed. That seed goes out into our future, takes root, and eventually brings a harvest of consequences, whether positive or negative, into our experience.

People often sow seeds of bad character, reap a harvest of negative consequences, and then point their finger at *others* and say, "You didn't come through for me!" People ruin their lives by their own foolish choices; yet, they are angry with others, blaming someone else over their own failure to exercise wise judgment.

As we become people of character, we will avoid this trap. If we choose to act with integrity, we will pass our "character tests" and become genuine, positive influencers of others. **Our lives can beneficially influence others only to the degree that we are willing to walk in nobility of character.**

We must stay continually aware that the situations and circumstances

of life are testing us every moment of every day. It is how we *respond* to these tests of character (with either a positive or a negative response) that will determine the outcome of our lives.

From a negative perspective, tests come to discourage, deflate, or destroy us. On the positive side, they come in order to position us for a better and stronger future. Just as there is no opportunity for advancement without a final exam, there is no triumph without a proving ground. **Good character is not the *goal* but, rather, the *key* that unlocks the door to fulfilling life's purpose.**

It is wise to not despise the testing grounds of life. A test is merely an objective tool by which we are drawn into the Universal Law of Sowing and Reaping. That law is timeless and unchanging; it will be in operation as long as the earth remains. Like the Law of Gravity, the Law of Sowing and Reaping has been perpetually set in motion, and there is nothing you or I can do to change it.

We have the opportunity to change the natural course of our lives by sowing seeds of character. Whatever seeds we sow, whether good or bad, that is the kind of harvest we will reap. Many say, "It doesn't matter what I do; I will be fine." But that isn't true. A lack of character will always produce unwanted consequences.

What Does the Future Hold?

That's the issue, friend — *character.* How long are we willing to stand? Are we willing to live, for the rest of our lives, under the pressure that comes from holding fast to what is right and true? If so, the door of an unlimited, positive future will remain open. Yes, we will face many difficult obstacles. But even in the midst of adversity, we will continue

to rise to ever-higher levels of excellence and favor, as long as we do not stop sowing the right seed.

We only get out of life what we are willing to put into it. The earth is programmed to bring forth a multiplication of what we sow. People or circumstances may try to stand in our way, but nothing can stop our harvest from coming forth. All we have to do is put our seed in the ground and leave it there, no matter what winds of adversity blow against us. As we do, the Law of Sowing and Reaping will work — not part of the time but *all* the time.

The problem is, we live in a microwave society in which people expect instant answers. Too often, we wonder, waver, and ultimately pull our good seed out of the ground, because things aren't happening as quickly as we think they should. As a result, we stand in danger of canceling out our moment of change!

It is imperative to realize that it is our character that causes the recompense of our hands to come to us. If our character is good, then good will come into our lives from the good deposit we have made. If our character is bad, that toxicity will bring forth destruction in our lives, as a function of the Law of Sowing and Reaping. We may think that we can disregard this law and, somehow, still be successful. But how can we expect to reap a harvest of favor and success from seed we have never sown? There isn't a farmer in the world who believes he can reap a harvest where he has never sown a seed!

Sowing and Reaping

Sowing and reaping are the governors of destiny. The landscape of history is littered with the decayed remnants of once powerful nations that

were destroyed, not by some ruthless invader but by the hand of their own choices. As the ancient Roman Empire rose to greatness, its leaders reveled and romped in unparalleled power and prosperity. They no doubt expected their superiority and influence to continue for centuries. Yet, even as they basked in their wealth, they were sowing seeds that would culminate in their ruin. Leaders began to hoard and misuse the wealth, while the common people fought hunger and unemployment. People discarded their moral values and self-respect. Growing numbers believed that breaking the law was justified, as long as it "helped" them. This "end-justifies-the-means" mentality opened the door for even more lawlessness. And so historians record "The Rise and Fall of the Roman Empire."[1]

Here is a similar, modern-day example. On January 22, 1973, the U.S. Supreme Court legalized unrestricted abortion in America. Immediately, thousands of babies began to be aborted. Since that landmark decision, there have been more than 49 million abortions performed in the United States.[2] The number of babies that are annually aborted is now more than 1.37 million in the USA, and 46 million globally. Those babies who were aborted in 1973 would be almost forty years old today.

In the United States, there is presently a national outcry about the fact that the Social Security system is in trouble. But think about all the lost revenue that would have been deposited into Social Security by the millions who have been aborted since the early 1970's. The very people who passed the law to kill unborn children will not be taken care of in their old age, largely as a result of that decision!

Make no mistake, friend — the Law of Sowing and Reaping is supreme in the universe. We must never fool ourselves into believing that we can escape the harvest from the careless seeds that we have sown.

But what about an example of someone who chose to sow the *right*

seed? Let's consider the life of Peter Daniels, a rags-to-riches international businessman and statesman from Australia. Born into a poor family, in the midst of the Great Depression of the 1930's, Peter was familiar with the harsh, cold realities of poverty. As an illiterate, impoverished bricklayer, he began to sow what he could into those around him. Never withholding the little that he had, Peter sowed precious seeds of compassion, time, and generosity, which held a future harvest beyond anything that he could imagine or dream.

Though failing in business a number of times, he started to gain financial momentum as he continued to sow into the lives of others. Doors of favor began to open; eventually, this unlearned bricklayer became a sought-after entrepreneur, business consultant, motivational speaker, and multi-millionaire.

Though his conditions and surroundings have changed immensely since those poor days as a bricklayer, two distinct threads can be seen to run consistently through the rich tapestry of his life — **his impeccable integrity and his prolific generosity.** Though now approaching his eighties, he still travels the world, conducting high-profile business seminars and training young entrepreneurs. These meetings are often free of charge, with Mr. Daniels financially providing the whole program, the follow-up meal, his own travel expenses, and donating any funds raised.

Those who have had the incredible honor of sowing their precious seed into this honorable man have seen their lives exponentially increased, as a result. When we sow into the field of an upright man, we don't even have to know what we're doing. We'll come out on top because *he knows* what he is doing!

Begin with a Decision

As we discussed previously, **pursuing excellent character always begins with a decision.** Let's determine that we *will* be people of character, no matter what anyone else says or does. When things get hard, we must choose to stand on principles, rather than throw in the towel and give up.

That's why it is so important to find trustworthy people of character with whom to associate. Sadly, in this day and age, that is not always easy to do.

It is interesting to read books that were written at least a hundred years ago. Once the reader gets past the "Queen's English," he often begins to see the authors' depth of character, even when he has no previous knowledge of them.

When reading speeches of men such as Winston Churchill and Abraham Lincoln, one is struck by the wisdom and strong character exhibited in some of the statements they made. The same is true when reading the works of some of America's founding fathers. When comparing their words to the present generation, a person can't help but think, *"My, how things have changed! Instead of thinking it strange when we find a person who DOESN'T have character, we think it's strange when we find a person who DOES!"*

The number of scholastic degrees a person has will often take second place to what he has done in life to develop his *character.* When someone breaks the back of generations of bondage and blight, the world takes notice.

I remember one woman who stood up during a meeting and said, "I'm a fifth-generation welfare recipient, but I just want to let everyone know that I'll never again be on welfare."

That woman forever changed the future for herself and her children, when she made that courageous stand and said, "No more. Those days are over." A person like that both inspires and deserves respect. Those are the types of individuals we all want to associate with, during our time on earth.

A person's good character will not allow him to be denied. It will compel people to deal with him. When he walks into a room, some will think, "Why does this person irritate me so?" They won't be irritated because he has done something wrong. They will be irritated because he is a person who does *what is right.*

We must be more interested in building our own good character than we are in exposing the lack of character in others. Let's give others the liberty to straighten out their own lives, while we evaluate our condition. We should each carefully examine who we are, as well as what we think, do, and say in our daily lives, allowing the inner searchlight of our conscience to reveal any areas of needed adjustments. As we do, a day *will* come when the seeds of character we have chosen to sow will produce an abundant harvest of honor and benefit in our lives, beyond our greatest expectations!

JUST REMEMBER, GARFIELD, WHEN WE GET TO THE FARM YOU ARE THERE TO RELAX
JIM DAVIS
3-30

I KNOW LAST TIME YOU WANTED TO BE HELPFUL...

BUT YOU DO NOT GROW CHICKENS BY PLANTING CHICKENS IN THE GROUND!
IT WAS AN HONEST MISTAKE
© 1981 PAWS, INC. All Rights Reserved.

There Is No Escape

Chapter 6

MAHOUT CONVENTION

". . . and nobody noticed the elephant in the room."

As people go through life, many do not recognize the consequences that result from their actions. It is easy to forget that the decisions we make today could forever change our lives, our families' lives, and the lives of several generations to come.

Studies have been conducted through entire family trees, tracing the consequences of one individual's poor choice, such as the decision to start drinking alcohol, to abuse drugs, or to engage in sexual promiscuity. When an individual makes a bad decision, he may think it is all over as soon as he completes the deed. But that single poor choice often continues to produce a devastating harvest, long after that person is dead and gone.

Some time ago, the state of New York did a study on five generations of the Edwards family. I have read differing reports on the number of influential family members, so I will generalize it a bit. In those five generations that were studied, the researchers were able to trace 729 male descendants. Out of these 729, two hundred became preachers, sixty-five became Bible college teachers, thirteen were university presidents, and sixty were authors. Scores of them held public office, and more than one hundred were lawyers and judges. Sixty were doctors, a few were senators and governors, and one was a vice president. All this issued from one man and woman who loved God and set themselves to raise their children for God. We can see, from these statistics, how many sanctifying seeds were sown from that determined couple.[1]

At the same time, the state of New York did a similar study of an

ungodly posterity. This study is worthy of our focus because it is a good example of what happens if we neglect our responsibilities. Max Juke and his brother married sisters. They were not Christians and rejected the teachings of the Bible. They believed in living their lives for themselves and going their own way. As with the Edwards family, five generations of their descendants were calculated. Of their 1,026 descendants (both male and female), three hundred spent an average of thirteen years each in the penitentiary. One hundred ninety of their descendants became public prostitutes, and one hundred were alcoholics. It was calculated, back in 1900, that it cost the state of New York $1.2 million to take care of all these wayward people. What a stark contrast to the virtuous and influential descendants of the Edwards family![1]

Simply put, **today's decisions determine tomorrow's circumstances, not only for us but for generations to follow.** Let's think about that for just a moment. How have our past decisions brought us to where we are today? If we have made some poor choices in the past, what right choices can we make, today, that would help us to get our lives back on track? Bad decisions cannot be fixed by counseling or some other form of "mental massage." Bad decisions can only be fixed by good decisions. But it requires *character* to be transparent enough to acknowledge a bad decision, and then ask for wisdom and direction.

Principle vs. Relationships

Many of us have experienced negative consequences in our lives as a result of esteeming a person above principle. We have made decisions based on our love for another person, even when those decisions violated our commitment to integrity and character.

Our commitment to integrity must never be destroyed by our love for another. We cannot allow our focus to be on others' opinions, on their failures, or on what they did or didn't do. If, instead, we focus on the unchanging standards of ethics and principle, we will, most often, make the right decisions.

Too often, we embrace this principle only when we want to do something different than what our authorities have directed. That's when we claim, "I can't allow my personal conscience to be violated." But we forget that authority structures have been established for both our *protection* and our *provision*.

There will be situations that arise in life that we may not necessarily be prepared to handle. But if we will listen to the authorities that have been placed in our lives, we will be able to glean wisdom from them and, thus, come through each situation safely.

The Root of Every Problem

The problems that you and I are facing right now — whether disease, financial lack, feelings of insecurity, low self-esteem, or vices that have plagued our families for generations — all have their origin in lack of character. Someone chose to love the way of compromise more than he or she loved the way of character.

That is the way it works in this life. My character matters to you. Your character matters to me. What we do in this life matters greatly to others, for our actions produce consequences far beyond the small circle of our own lives.

We must daily ask ourselves:

- *Where am I allowing poor character in my life?*
- *Have I made a poor choice that needs to be fixed today?*
- *Am I compromising principle for the love of a person?*
- *Does lack of character have anything to do with my lack of progress?*

Can't Avoid It

History records that the ancient Israelite king, David, was a man who had a heart for truth and virtue. He was a leader who brought his people back to a love for character.

But one day, he chose not to walk in the very integrity he demanded from others. Instead of going to battle with his men, he stayed home, went out on his rooftop, and looked down upon a woman bathing; it was his friend's wife, Bathsheba. Then he went out to watch her the next day, and the next — until his desire grew so ferocious within him that he took Bathsheba for himself.

David understood what his poor character choice meant. He knew that **character pursues doing what is right, not what is comfortable.** He knew he couldn't walk in integrity *and* have that woman. But David refused to listen to the guiding principles within him and went his own way. As a result, he was a man entangled in compromise and self-deception for nearly a year.

Finally, someone who cared for the king went to him and helped him recognize his violation of character. When David realized what he had done, he was grieved and had a deep change of heart; nonetheless, he still lost his newborn son by Bathsheba, as a consequence of his poor choices.

Many times we don't really know what is wrong in our lives until someone comes and tells us. We don't recognize what's happening until someone loves us enough to tell us the truth. *But the question is, will we listen and respond to that wise instruction when it is given to us?*

Even when others choose deception, character refuses to compromise truth. However, we have to remember that there is one person we can never help: *the person who has no standard of truth.* Instead of listening to what truth has to say, he will try to drag you into an argument. The English philosopher, John Locke, once noted, "It's one thing to show a man that he is in error, and another to put him in possession of truth."

We should, however, never back away from compassionately speaking the truth, for that truth may be the only way of escape for someone caught in a snare of self-deception and compromised character.

Let's consider an example of a man named Ahithophel, who triggered destructive consequences for himself and others, because he did not speak the truth to a person who needed to hear it.

Ahithophel was King David's chief advisor — a friend he had known since childhood. He loyally served and counseled David, and was quite close to the king and his family.

David's son, Absalom, was a handsome man who had always been popular with the people. Absalom knew all the right things to say, in order to appear wise. But in reality, Absalom was secretly rebelling against his father.

As king of a great nation, David had to make certain decisions that some of his people did not understand. David's son, Absalom, was right there, to take advantage of the people's misgivings, by drawing their allegiance away from David and unto himself.

David's best friend, Ahithophel, was aware of Absalom's sedition. But, instead of going to Absalom and confronting the young man with the truth about his rebellion, Ahithophel actually went over to Absalom's side and, as a result, almost destroyed David's kingship.

David wrote the following words, at a time when he was facing opposition from both Absalom and Ahithophel, two of the people he loved most:

> Confuse them, Lord, and frustrate their plans,
>   for I see violence and conflict in the city.
> Its walls are patrolled day and night against invaders,
>   but the real danger is *wickedness within* the city.[2]

Another word for the phrase *wickedness within*, in the above passage, is the word *guile*. Guile occurs inside an individual when the seat of his life has become crooked. A person with guile is a fraudulent person, a double-talker. He may talk well of you to your face, but behind your back he will leave little hints of doubt about you. He may not say anything overtly negative, but somehow he finds a way to plant seeds of distrust about you in the minds of others. This is what Absalom did in Ahithophel's relationship with the king — until finally Absalom succeeded in pulling Ahithophel away from David, his closest friend.

David's grief over Ahithophel's betrayal can be felt in these words:

> It is not an enemy who taunts me —
>   I could bear that.
> It is not my foes who so arrogantly insult me —
>   I could have hidden from them.
> Instead, it is you — my equal,
>   my companion and close friend.
> What good fellowship we once enjoyed...

> As for my companion, he betrayed his friends;
> he broke his promises.
> His words are as smooth as butter,
> but in his heart is war.
> His words are as soothing as lotion,
> but underneath are daggers![3]

Consider what could have happened had Ahithophel gone to the younger man and counseled him, "Absalom, don't do this. You're making a mistake, son." Perhaps Absalom would have listened to his father's friend, choosing not to betray his father. We will never know, because Ahithophel chose the way of poor character and turned against his best friend.

Ahithophel did not escape the consequences of his poor decision. The day came when Absalom also betrayed him, refusing his advice and publicly disgracing him. The betrayal that Ahithophel sowed became the harvest that he reaped. He was so devastated that he hanged himself. The Universal Law of Sowing and Reaping had caught up to him: **The seed one sows today is the harvest he will reap tomorrow.**

The same principle holds true in our lives. How many negative consequences have we suffered because, as a function of our own poor character, we wouldn't listen to wisdom or choose the right course?

In November 1998, news headlines reported that a Harvard Divinity School dean had suddenly stepped down from his post, claiming it was for "personal and professional reasons." In May of 1999, the Boston Globe reported the rest of the sad story. Technicians, who had been hired by the theologian to do some updating of his university-owned home computer, had found thousands of pornographic images and had informed Harvard officials. The dean had been forced to resign.

When this respected man was making the choice to download those pornographic images, did he expect to one day be exposed? Certainly not! But it did come to light, as all things eventually do. And the result was a stained career and reputation, not to mention the disillusionment of hundreds of students and faculty who looked up to him as an example of good character.

How often do we recklessly make poor choices, somehow believing that they will be without consequence? Sad to say, the consequences always come! But even in the midst of the fallout from a bad decision, we can be grateful that consequences and truth are training us in character, as we keep a teachable heart and embrace instruction.

A person who refuses to be molded in character is gambling with his future. There are serious consequences for those who insist on remaining stubborn and unteachable. If we refuse to be trained in character, life will become tormenting.

Training Ground

However painful the consequences of our wrong choices may be, they can be used to get us back on track with the plan for our lives. That is why we make a huge mistake when we bail someone out of a consequence they are facing due to poor character. In doing so, we are simply extending the life of their poor character and the resulting destruction. Although it is difficult, we must **refuse to obstruct consequences that come to the life of another.**

Our greatest desire may be to stop the pain that someone else is going through. But if that person never experiences the painful consequences of his poor character choices, he may never learn or grow.

The same thing is true when a wife tries to stop her husband from disciplining the children. As the husband gets ready to punish disobedient behavior, the wife cries, "No, no, don't do that!" In standing between the children and their father, she prevents them from experiencing the consequences of their disobedient actions. Instead of learning obedience, the children learn that if they make poor choices, mom will always be there to protect them from the corresponding backlash!

When we, as parents, do not take our rightful position in the disciplining of our children, consequences will step in to do it for us, by bringing the negative harvest of our children's disobedience. If we insist on stepping in to "protect" them from their consequences, we will likely stop the very process that will ensure the transformation that they so desperately need. And if we continue to tolerate compromise and rebellion in our children, over a long period of time, we are in danger of seeing the day when they will be destroyed — without remedy.

None of us want to see our children fail. But we must realize that they can only succeed and prosper as they learn to follow after character. It is our responsibility to teach our children what we, too, must learn: **A lack of character reaps an unwanted future.** There is no substitute for character — *absolutely none!*

We have to learn the difference between assistance (helping a person who is down) and *interference* (attempting to circumvent a person's consequences). We must not stop consequences from coming to another person. If we bail him out, he will never learn or grow in character; and it won't be long before he's in the same jam all over again. Why is this true? Because, **when we refuse to learn by instruction, consequences will readily take its place.**

A lack of character is the reason that, in years gone by, the lives of several tremendously gifted men and women ended hideously. We have often discounted the greatness of these fallen individuals because of the way their lives ended. Yet, no one can deny the exceptional accomplishments of their earlier years.

So why did their lives end the way they did? Why did they bring no fruit to maturity? Because they lacked strength of character. They refused to live their lives in a principled manner. Thus, they made themselves open game for destruction. This can all be summed up by the following principle: **When our entire focus is on getting what we want, we will eventually lose what we had.**

Once we start recognizing the consequences of bad character, it is easy to see why character is such an important issue. We must raise our standards high, for without them, we are as those who build houses on shifting sand.

"Think of it as a legal loophole."

Standing The Test Of Time

Chapter 7

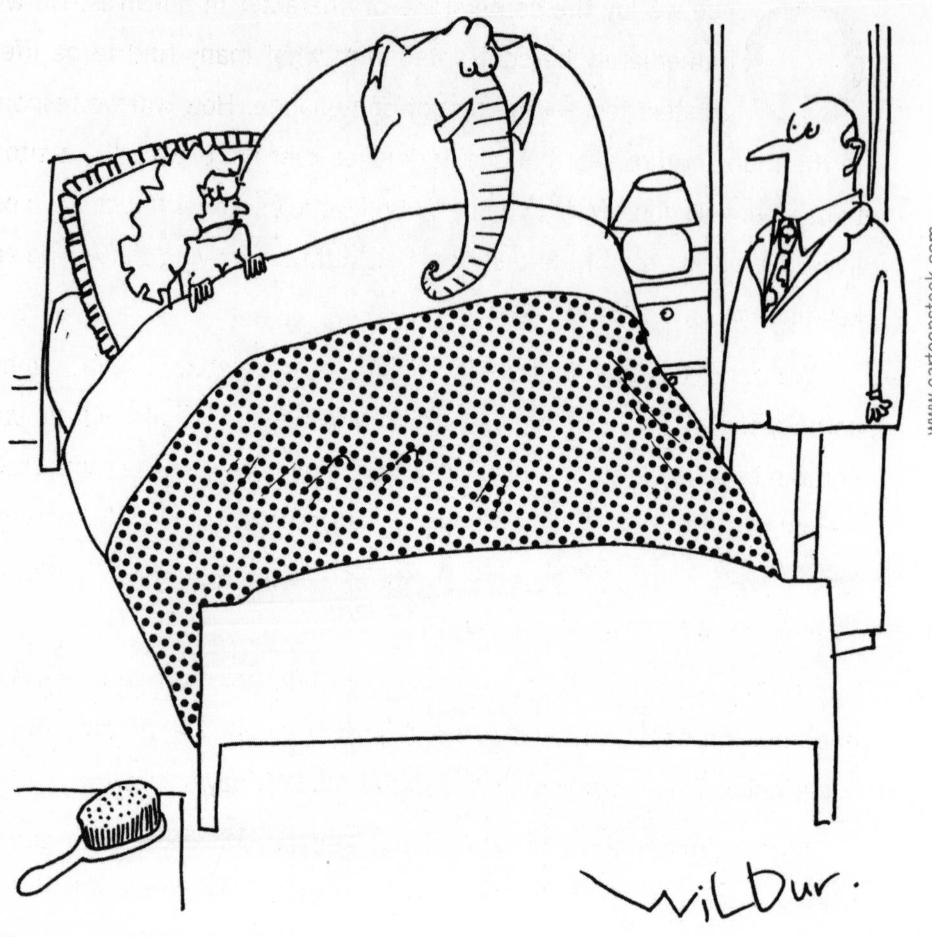

THE ELEPHANT IN THE ROOM

Once we lay the cornerstone of character in our lives, we will immediately be confronted with what many find to be life's greatest test — the test of compliance. How will we respond to the many authorities that society places over us, especially in situations where we don't want to comply? Will we reject *the influencers* in our lives? Or will we stand the test of time, faithfully serving those who are key links to our future success?

We cannot ignore this subject, for until we set this foundational cornerstone firmly in place, everything else we try to build will be vulnerable to collapse and failure. The moment we start getting somewhere — just about the time when promotion arrives — disrespect for authorities will knock down what we have worked so hard to build, taking us back to the beginning of our journey.

In the arena of developing character, the issue of relating to influencers is perhaps the most difficult to comprehend and apply in our experience. This is especially true in our modern-day society.

Many individuals, both the young and adults alike, have gotten sucked into a self-centered, rebellious mindset. They assume they can violate proven codes of ethics, yet escape the consequences of their selfish actions. But **true character refuses to rob its future in order to enjoy its present.**

Here is what many people fail to understand: Everything in the realm of sowing and reaping takes time — and a lot of it. There is a prolonged

season of sowing seed, and there is a prolonged season of reaping the harvest. However, because there is a prolonged harvest, a person often won't notice the cause-and-effect connection between the seed he sowed years ago and the negative consequences he is currently reaping. He doesn't realize he is experiencing a harvest from his own past seeds of character violations. The reaping has been so long in coming that he doesn't put the two together.

But, as we've previously discussed, the Universal Law of Sowing and Reaping cannot be ignored, disregarded, dodged, or by-passed. This law says we *will* reap what we sow; and whether it's sooner or later makes little difference.

When it comes to compliance to authority, the trump card often used by willful and headstrong people is the word "control." When they don't want to do what delegated authority has suggested that they do, they lash out with the accusation, "You're just trying to control me!"

But a person of **character recognizes compliance as an instrument for good in life, rather than an instrument of control.** When a person in a leadership position asks someone in a lower position to do something, and that request is rooted in moral principle, is that leader controlling the other person? No, for his desire is to be an influencer — to lead that person to do right and receive the rewards of doing right. The leader is only operating in his delegated position as an instrument in helping that person become all that he can be.

NOT CONTROL

Rulers and authorities are not a threat to those who do what is right. The only people who are intimidated or fearful of authority are those who do things they know are wrong. If we want to be free from the fear of authority, we simply need to do what is right, with a good attitude; then, our leadership will commend us.

Leaders have been placed in their positions of authority *for our benefit.* They are there to compensate the people who do right; but if we choose to be rebellious and noncompliant, we should be concerned, for they have been given full authority to deal with our recalcitrance.

These principles of compliance apply to every area of life — our workplaces, our marriages, our children, and our citizenship. Why are there so many breakdowns in relationship? Because people rebel against the structures of safety that have been instituted!

Civil authority is beneficial to society, because order is the only way a society can thrive. Order is essential to all life. For example, cells in the human body that reproduce incorrectly are called cancerous. They have gotten out of order and, therefore, must be removed to save the individual's life. Authority is assigned to bring that essential order to our lives. Its desire is not to take away our freedom but to help us avoid mistakes and harm. Are all people in authority good? No, certainly not, but that is not the issue. I am referring to us. What is our responsibility? That is the real issue.

PRINCIPLES OF POSTURE

We have been given a posture, or an attitude to assume, in every relationship in life. That posture is our link to *favor.* Therefore, when entering a new relationship, we have to understand who we are, within that particular relationship, and how to relate. Then we must posture ourselves in the relationship, according to the responsibility that we have been given.

Character discovers its assignment in every relationship and then postures itself accordingly. For instance, a corporate executive cannot act with the same authority before his company president that he does when he stands before his own office staff. He must assume two different postures, because these are two different types of relationships. He goes before his staff making statements; but he walks before his president asking questions. Why? Not because the president has greater inherent value, as a person, but simply because he governs the executive's position, as his delegated authority. We are to be *subject* to our respective bosses. That word "subject" means we are *to bow our own desires to theirs.* Sound impossible? This concept will become clearer, as we explore further.

The correct posture becomes much easier to assume when we determine to stay faithful to *principle*, not necessarily to people. For instance, you or I may get upset with people, but we don't have the right to spout off at them. We must relate to others according to *our* internal character barometer, not according to their actions.

Virtue does not require that one be eloquent, innovative, or skillful in leadership abilities. However, it does require that one be *faithful.* The goal isn't to be the slickest person on the block or the sharpest pencil in the box; the goal is simply to be found faithful.

When we look at this issue of relating to influencers, relationship

becomes very simple. Whatever position we hold determines the posture we are to take. It is equally as important to know *who we are not* as it is to know *who we are* in each and every relationship. When we understand our correct posture in relationship, we will ultimately be promoted.

The posture we are to assume in our relationships with our superiors doesn't change based upon how well they exercise their authority in our lives. Whether they are easy or challenging to follow, they still occupy the leadership position, and we still must relate to them according to ethical principles of compliance.

As I mentioned earlier, these principles are true in every realm of life. Whether we are husbands, wives, fathers, mothers, sons, daughters, employers, or employees, we will find a definition of who we are in the proven principles of integrity. When we don't understand the role we have, in a particular relationship, we miss out on its many benefits and bring upon ourselves all kinds of frustration and consequences. We must define who we are in each of our relationships and then posture ourselves accordingly. **We will never find success in our pursuit of excellent character until we have taken this step.**

Respect Boundaries

Only a very small percentage of people even attempt to fulfill the appropriate roles in their relationships. For those who do, though, life becomes very simple. Such people are fulfilled and at peace. They stop looking over the fence, wishing they were someone else. Everything becomes easier when we understand the power of order and boundaries.

Any movement towards order, in one's personal life, will bring productivity and growth. Even the simplest step toward order can make an

enormous difference. For instance, the moment a person refuses to leave his bedroom in the morning without first making the bed, he has taken a step toward a life that is defined by order.

When we understand the importance of defining parameters in life, we don't try to mold the people around us into what we want them to be. Instead, we try to encourage people to be the unique, special individuals that they are. When they feel comfortable and confident stepping into their specific roles and distinct identities, they are much more willing to adapt themselves to the authority figures in their lives.

Jurisdictions

Every authority has a jurisdiction. "Jurisdiction" can be defined as *authority and power, based on right.* In other words, jurisdiction refers to *authorized power and responsibility.* It also refers to those areas and spheres over which such authority can be exercised — defined boundaries that are not to be violated. That means there are people who have authority and jurisdiction in one area of our lives, but none in other areas.

Upon close examination, we will find that the majority of conflicts in our personal lives, in business, in diplomacy, and in most other societal relations comes as a direct result of jurisdictional violations.

It is imperative that we remember two key principles when dealing with matters of jurisdiction:

1. We must each be diligent to discover, understand, and fulfill all our responsibilities within our given jurisdiction(s).
2. We must never cross another's jurisdictional boundaries.

Those with honorable character refuse to take authority over something that they are not responsible for. That is why someone such as our previously discussed corporate executive doesn't allow himself to get dragged into the family matters of his staff. Unless ethical violations are being committed that will affect others within his responsibility, he does not have jurisdiction in their personal family matters and should refuse to extend his jurisdiction where he does not have the responsibility to do so.

Conflicting Commands

It is necessary that we understand matters of jurisdiction, so we can know what to do when we face conflicting instructions, coming from different directions. The first question to ask ourselves in such a situation is this: *Does this person have the right to give me this command?* Once the answer to that question is deciphered, it becomes much easier to answer the next: *Should I listen to this person's instructions, concerning this situation?*

For example, let's say we are commanded by a governmental authority to carry out an action that is a blatant violation of the fundamental respect for human life. Even though duty calls upon us to submit to governmental authorities, in this case we must submit to an even higher authority — the moral and ethical responsibility to protect human life. Because jurisdictional boundaries have been crossed, we must follow our moral compass above all. **When asked to violate principles, a person of character chooses to comply with his ethical integrity.**

Violating Principle

Let's look at the steps we should take if someone in charge asks us to do something contrary to our own moral conscience. First, *we must discipline our own poor attitude.* You see, as soon as we're asked to do something unethical, that request immediately elicits a response from us. If our response is also unethical, we suddenly become as guilty as the person who instructed us to do something wrong.

Secondly, *we must continue to walk in integrity and respect toward others.* As we commit to demonstrate excellence in both attitude and job performance, our integrity will eventually deliver us to the other side of every difficult situation, with our character unviolated and intact.

Finally, *we must appeal to those in positions of authority on the basis of ethical principle.* For the most part, superiors really appreciate it when someone appeals to them with established principles of truth and honor. People who appeal with their opinions and their attitudes rarely have much to say. However, if all of us will bow to truth, we'll arrive at a peaceable solution in every situation.

Compliance Is a Decision

We should continually strive to live from our inner character compass and not according to the capricious customs of society. If we will do this, we won't have to be constantly corrected or restrained by others. Instead, we will be *self-correctors* who know right from wrong and choose to honor ethical principle, even in the most challenging of situations.

Whenever we willingly listen to the influencers who have been placed over us, character is the harvest that our lives will produce. Why? Be-

cause those over us will often ask us to do things we don't desire to do, and character is developed only as we willingly fulfill those unwanted assignments.

If we are interested in productivity in our lives, we must choose the path of compliance: **for the fruit of compliance is character; the fruit of character is moral strength; and the effect of moral strength is productivity.**

Respect the Position

Character responds to positions of leadership with honor and respect. This doesn't necessarily mean that every individual who is in a leadership position is worthy of honor and respect by merit of his *person*. He is, however, due that respect and honor by merit of the *position* that he holds. For instance, in the realm of government, there are offices and positions that must be held in high esteem for the influence they hold and the policy decisions they will make in countless lives. In turn, it is our responsibility to make right choices regarding who fills such positions, so we can live in peace and our children can live in safety.

We demonstrate a glaring lack of character when we judge others, especially our leaders! The truth is that whenever we criticize others, we condemn ourselves, for those who point fingers at others are usually practicing the same vices.

Something else that must be considered is that our leaders were not placed in their positions to please *us*. They were placed there to serve and please *their authorities*. Who are we, then, to criticize another man's responsibility? They are accountable to *their* authorities, not to us! **A man of character refuses to circumvent the structure of authority that he has been assigned to obey.**

SABOTAGING OUR PROMOTIONS

Those in charge of certain areas of our lives have the ability to give both demotions and promotions to those who are under their jurisdictions. When a person attempts to forge ahead with his own plans, without the approval or oversight of those who are leading, he circumvents authority and sabotages both the *protective advantage of accountability* and the *promotional advantage of favor.*

Now, we may wish it didn't work this way, but that doesn't change anything. This principle holds true no matter how many people float in and out of commitments and relationships, saying, "Well, I'm my own person, and I don't need to be accountable to anyone." That faulty way of thinking is still a lie, no matter how many people believe it.

Some people focus so much on their individuality and independence that they reject all authorities in life. However, such behavior is a perversion of individual rights. True, each person has individual rights, but not the right to do whatever he or she wants. Rather, each person has a right to do what is ethical.

REWARDS OR CONSEQUENCES? *IT'S OUR CHOICE*

Remember, **the choices we make are the only factors that decide whether we will be overtaken with rewards or consequences.** The consequences of our choices cannot be changed or altered; those consequences are dictated by the Law of Sowing and Reaping. If we choose to be noncompliant and self-willed, our choice has an emotional hand grenade tied to it. That ticking bomb will eventually explode and bring destruction into our lives and, possibly, the lives of those around us.

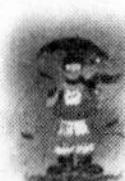

A biblical prophet said these words: "If you are willing and obedient, you shall eat the best of the land." Many people want to have the best of everything, but aren't experiencing anything of the sort. Here's why: *They are not willing to honor those in charge.* The moment a leader has a conversation with them about something that could be altered, they consider it a lecture and quickly become disrespectful.

A Time-Honored Advocate

Many people grew up in dysfunction, where authority figures hurt and abused them. In order to protect themselves, they hardened and closed their hearts. Even as adults, they carry the belief that authority figures will hurt and abuse them, if given the chance.

However, ethical authority is an *advocate* and an *asset* in our lives, sent to reward us when we are compliant and to get us back on track when we go astray.

Why is it so important to understand this? Because, if we don't adjust our thinking in this area, we will be hindered in every arena of life. But, if we start relating to our authorities as proponents for our good, we will be protected when we make errors in judgment. We will be delivered out of the messes we make for ourselves, just by virtue of our compliant hearts.

We cannot remain disrespectful and closed off to leadership and then expect to be rescued from self-imposed difficulties. After all, disrespect was the source of our problems in the first place!

Pass the Test

There is only one way to extricate ourselves from the mire of disrespect and dishonor: We must rise above it by listening to precepts of truth rather than to our own misguided perspectives.

It is our choice. We must choose, for ourselves, whether or not we are going to comply. If we pass the tests, by making the right choices to willingly comply with authoritative directives, we will begin to see a dramatic transformation take place in our lives. We will rid ourselves of fear, we will feel safer than ever before, and joy will return to our lives in abundant measure. In other words, we will eat the best of the land!

ARE WE THERE YET? ARE WE THERE YET? ARE WE THERE YET? ARE WE THERE YET? ARE WE THERE YET? ARE WE THERE YET? ARE WE THERE...
THE MOST SEVERE TEST OF PIONEER ENDURANCE
DIST. BY UNIVERSAL PRESS SYNDICATE WILEY@NON-SEQUITUR.COM
WILEY©03 7-5 WWW.UCOMICS.COM

Don't Bend The Truth

Chapter 8

"No, this is the elephant."

In our society, where ethical relativism runs rampant, truthfulness remains one of the foundational bedrocks of life. **It is simply not possible to walk in character without a lifelong commitment to live by the truth.**

We cannot be happy or at peace unless we embrace truth in our innermost being. But before we can do that, we must first understand what truth really *is*. Truth, in its purest form, can only be defined by a standard far higher than man's.

The word "truth" comes from the Hebrew word *emeth*, which means *stability; certainty; [that which is] right and sure*. It is derived from another word, *aman*, which means *to build up or support; to foster as a parent or a nurse; to be firm and faithful; or to be permanent, steadfast, and verifiable.*

The dictionary says that truth includes the qualities of *loyalty, trustworthiness, sincerity, genuineness, and honesty.* Honesty is *the quality of being in accordance with the facts of reality,* and *the possession of an agreement with a standard.*

Setting a standard of truth in our lives is extremely important if we are to walk in ethical character. This implies that the established truths of life are *never negotiable*, and we maintain a habitual adherence to accuracy in every situation.

Truth isn't according to the way you or I see it. Truth is according to the unchanging, immovable principles of the universe. We have to be

willing to acknowledge when someone else acts on the truth, even when we are embarrassed about our own dishonesty. We must also be willing to admit when we have compromised the truth as a cover up for our own weaknesses.

So often, in relationships, we play games with others. We all silently agree not to discuss the elephant in the room — *the real issues.* Our secret hope is that, as long as no one discusses them, those issues do not exist.

But, somehow, it just doesn't work that way. The real issues *do* exist, whether we want to confront them or not. **Our shortcomings, weaknesses, and deceptions exist, even when we choose to avoid them, discount them, or pretend they are not there.** The principles of truth don't slide up and down a scale, like man's changing opinions and perspectives. Regardless of what we do with truth, it remains an unchanging standard that continues throughout time.

So often, people spend their time trying to look better than they really are, rather than simply walking in transparency and truth! That is why we must be interested in the standards of those who surround us. We need to examine every assumption *in light of the principles of truth.* If we find that something isn't true, we must challenge it, because we are interested in truth and honesty, not in the traditions of humanity.

How do we accelerate our own personal pursuit of truth? Men and women of character continually return to principles of ethics and integrity for their supply of truth. If we choose to disregard truth, our lives are then built on shifting sand. At all junctures, we must endeavor to be truthful — both with ourselves as well as with others.

A truthful individual is one who is completely void of all guile and deception. "Guile" is the very antithesis of truth. Though we briefly

discussed this word earlier, let's take a closer look at what it means.

Guile is more than a lie. A person of guile is someone who has systematically set up a framework of lies in his mind. That framework has become so established that it now defines the way he portrays himself in real life. He has told these lies to himself and to others so often that he now believes they are the truth.

This is a person who has begun to believe his own "press releases." He sees things only from his own perspective. In fact, in a way, he has set *himself* up as being or portraying truth. While living his life under this deception, he is unable to access the enormous power of real truth.

The Power of Truth

There is great power in truth, for truth is the road to continual, lasting change, resulting in promotion. It will never let us down. When we live in truth, we never have to remember what we lied about. We can allow the positive traits of transparency and vulnerability to bring favor into our lives and catapult us to increase and growth. We soon come to realize that **excellence in life can only be achieved when we embrace truth as the only avenue to promotion.**

Every one of us must keep ourselves in check. We cannot afford to step out of truth, even for a moment, for the older we get, the more our deceptions affect others. The more influential we become, the more our influence will trickle down to future generations. *What we say matters.* One lie is one too many! One omission of truth is too much. **Character looks to truth to be the most celebrated influencer in its life.**

Yes, there is power in truth — but what exactly does truth do for us in this life?

1. **Truth forces darkness into the light.**
2. **Truth is the internal compass that guides our actions.**
3. **Truth protects us from the deception and destructive results of situational ethics.**
4. **Truth causes us to be pursued by others with favor and promotion.**
5. **Truth is the preservation of leaders.**

Finding Truth

How can we learn the truth? First, we have to understand this about ourselves: Our natural tendency is to accept false ideas and be drawn toward what is wrong. We have a *propensity toward deception.* Bad decisions actually appeal to our human reasoning (although, at the time, we cannot or will not see that these decisions will lead to bad relationships, poverty, illness, or even death). Many behaviors and ways that actually seem right and reasonable to an individual can eventually lead to his demise.

The bottom line is that we are easily deceived. That's why the intake of ethical principles and undiluted absolutes is such a vital habit to cultivate, in our pursuit of excellent character. Consistent intake of truth, every day, every day, *every day,* is the only thing that will bring us to a point of success and tranquility in life.

Secondly, we must fill our souls (our minds, wills, and emotions) with truth. Any growth or increase that happens in our lives occurs via the soul. When an individual's mind, will, and emotions prosper, that pros-

perity then permeates every area of life, *from the inside out.* From the abundance of a person's heart, his mouth will speak. Those words of life will then spill out into the circumstances that surround him, causing each situation to line up with principles of truth.

Many people attempt to do it the opposite way. They think that just because they express a desire, that means they can have it. Unfortunately for them, it doesn't work that way. In regard to any area of life, a person has to continually take the nourishment of truth into his soul. As his soul becomes filled with information that brings faith to life, everything that is opposite to truth will be forced out of doors.

Thirdly, we must commit ourselves to discard every thought or reasoning that aligns itself against what we know to be true. Every moment of every day, we must diligently scrutinize our thoughts, making each one wholly obedient to truth, integrity, and ethical principle. We will quickly discover that **character defines itself by continually evaluating its progress in the light of truth.**

That is why we cannot focus on our outward circumstances. On the contrary, we must continually look within. Our circumstances do not dictate our thoughts — rather, it is our thoughts that will ultimately dictate our circumstances. **The principles residing within will become the barometer of what will happen on the outside.** We will see excellent character and good success come to our lives as long as we keep filling our souls with truth and refuse to quit!

Examining Our Commitment

The following is a very effective checklist in determining one's personal level of commitment to truth. It would greatly benefit each of us to ask ourselves these questions on a regular basis.

1. Do I trust anyone enough to allow them to point out my blind spots?

We all have blind spots in different areas of our lives — weaknesses that we have no idea even exist. That is why we have to be willing to trust someone who loves us enough to point them out. We need to come to the place of trust that says, "If you say I have a blind spot that I'm not recognizing, then it must be true, because I know that you wouldn't lie to me. I'm going to take responsibility for it. I'm not going to deny it anymore."

2. Am I willing to confront the issues hidden by my blind spots?

Remember, we can never conquer what we are unwilling to confront. Every day we must each face our own giants (whether that giant is our past, a bad habit, or a particular weakness), determining that those giants will not steal even one hour from us, because we have made a quality decision to walk in truth!

3. Am I deceiving myself into believing that I am perfect and have no faults?

It is the easiest thing in the world to start looking for someone else to blame for the negative things that happen to us in life. But we need to be honest enough to point the finger of judgment back at ourselves and allow truth to show us where *we* need to change.

4. Do I think of myself more highly than I should think?

Knowing who we are is only half of what it takes to walk in truth. We also have to know who we are *not*, so we don't fall into the trap of pride and arrogance, which cause so many to live life as a lie.

5. Do I exaggerate my abilities?

We are to strive to be all that we've been created to be, no less and no more. We don't have to lie to prove our worth, for we've already been given great value and dignity. We need merely to walk in it.

6. Do I tell half-truths?

Most of us seldom tell the whole truth because of fear. We think if we don't tell all, we can escape consequences, avoid hurting someone, or protect ourselves from being hurt.

Truth is only truth when it is *all* the truth. We shouldn't delude ourselves into thinking that an omission of the truth is any less deceptive than a downright lie.

7. Do I flatter people to gain their approval?

Before directly answering this question, let's make a clarification. It is right for us to seek to please every person to whom we are accountable in life. If we are not actively solving their problems and making them feel good about their day, we are actually becoming a problem to them. *At any given moment, we are either problem-solvers or problem-creators.* Until we understand this particular principle of relating in life, we will never be able to walk in truth.

So what is the difference between flattery and a compliment? The difference is so slight that we won't hear it; we will only see it. Someone

who flatters does it because he *wants* something from the other person. Someone who compliments has no desire to take anything; he is looking to *give to that person.* Both people use exactly the same words, but their motives are different.

8. *Am I misrepresenting the principles I say I believe in, by harboring inconsistent or negative attitudes?*

When an individual rules his attitudes, he rules his heart. That is extremely significant. There is an old adage that says when a person can rule his own spirit, he is greater than one who can conquer a city. Think of it — if we learn how to rule our attitudes, we are indeed greater than four-star generals with armies at their command!

9. *Do I give damaging reports about others, in order to make myself look good?*

All these questions must be answered honestly if we are to cement the cornerstone of truth into our lives. Like King David of old, we must come to the place where we willingly say, "I have done wrong."

Each of us must go to the bedrock cornerstone of truth and, with honesty and sobriety, determine whether we have been walking in truth or believing lies. And *wherever* we find deception motivating our actions and attitudes, let's humble ourselves and make the needed changes. It's time to come face-to-face with ourselves and declare, "That attitude is *not* going to live here anymore. I will walk in truth, in all areas of my life!"

"You're right, the numbers don't lie. That's your job."

Section 2:

The Seven Pillars Of Character

Keep Your Cool

Pillar 1: Self-Control

“A person without self-control is as defenseless as a city with broken-down walls.”

- Book of Proverbs

Like computers, everything in life runs according to the rules of its operating system. There isn't any area of our lives that is inexplicable or that lacks an "owner's manual." And if we will embrace the rules that run the particular system in which we are pursuing excellence, we will reach our goal every time.

Many people run their lives on faulty operating systems. They have the idea that opportunities for promotion in life just happen. This is one of the first myths we must throw out of our minds, on our way to building a foundation of character. The truth is, doors of opportunity are sometimes slammed shut because of a failure in character.

Someone might seem like a person of good character on the outside, yet show a completely different side of himself when he goes home. No matter how he may appear to the outside world, this person's life will not produce the open doors he needs for success. You see, **when a person is one way on the outside and another way on the inside, he has no integrity.** It's only a matter of time before his faulty operating system will crash.

The Master Key

We now know that character is the foundational bedrock of a life of excellence. We also know that relinquishing our past and *choosing* to be new people are the first steps in building that foundation. *But is there a character key that unlocks the operating system — a character quality*

that governs and directs every other quality of excellent character?

Yes, this key is *self-control*. The word "self-control" means *to be strong, controlled, and restrained.* A person with self-control has mastery over his appetites, desires, physical urges, and emotions.

Without self-control, we will find ourselves continually falling short in the pursuit of character. Why is this? A lack of self-control speaks of our unwillingness to hang in there and endure for the long haul.

Far too often, we discard difficult relationships or abort challenging situations right at the point when we are about to win. Why? Because we govern our lives by an operating system of failure. In building foundations of character, most of us quickly discover that, if we have an issue with anyone, it is with our own tendencies toward failure. **The greatest giant one will ever face is himself.**

Keep in mind that in any race there are many runners, but only one person gets the prize. We must run in such a way that we will win! How? By employing self-control. All good athletes practice strict self-control. They run straight to the goal with purpose in every step.

We can't afford to be like boxers who miss their punches, or baseball players who can't hit the ball. We must discipline our actions like skilled athletes, training them to do what they should. Otherwise, we may find that, after helping others to win, *we ourselves* might be disqualified.

Mediocrity shuns this idea of restraint; but those who strive for the *mastery* practice strict self-control. They know that a lack of control is the greatest enemy to the pursuit of excellence.

Therefore, they live in the highest regard and respect for their inner conscience and the principles that guide it, while demonstrating love to those around them. They consider every thought, every word, and every

action, evaluating how it will affect others and how it will enhance or impair their productivity and their own sense of personal peace.

Even after discovering that we don't have to stay the way we were, we still have to find out what it would take to get us in a position to be changed. Initially, we don't need an exhaustive, line-by-line analysis of principles. First, we have to stop drowning in the whirlpool created by our own operating systems of defeat. Then we will be ready to hear more.

What do we have to do, in order to have our lives changed and re-arranged? Like athletes, we exercise self-control; we train and discipline our bodies. In other words, every time our selfish natures want to rise up, we slap them back down and say, "Get back down! You're not starting that mess again! All of that is over in my life."

Feed the Inner Man

So how do we establish the pillar of self-control and unlock a new operating system in our lives?

First, a person must recognize that his outer flesh and his inner conscience are at odds with one another. His outer man wants to act and respond in ways that his inner conscience knows is wrong. This is a constant inner struggle.

How can one make sure that the moral center of one's heart prevails in this daily struggle? Persistent meditation upon wise principles will give the inner man the incentive, strength, and tools it needs to consistently win this ongoing conflict.

But there will always be a struggle! One's outer man will come up with all kinds of ways to persuade him to neglect the very thing he needs most.

"I think I'll just wait till later to read and master a new principle."

"I'm just too busy, today, to study these precepts. I have so much going on right now. I know what I'll do. Tomorrow morning, I'll set the alarm for four o'clock and read two days' worth of that self-improvement book!"

It happens every time: **Our outer man tries to convince us to continually put off into the future what we know we need to do in the present.**

Always Symptoms

What can happen if we overrule the laziness and mediocrity of the outer man and begin to listen and respond to our inner conscience? We will begin to manifest several character traits in our lives:

LOVE: The Greek word for "love" is *agape. Agape* is a unique kind of love. It demonstrates love, regardless of feelings—even if a person doesn't deserve it, or is seemingly unworthy of being loved. This word *agape* is not something we feel; rather, it is *a love of reasoning or a love of the will.* In other words, when we sit back and consider the consequences of life, we choose to allow *love* to drive us, rather than bitterness or hatred. We *choose* to love, rather than to push for our own ways or try to protect ourselves.

JOY: This word "joy" refers to an *inner gladness* or a *deep-seated pleasure.* A person of joy has a depth of assurance and an inner gratitude that continually ignites a cheerful heart. That cheerfulness then permeates both his attitudes and his behavior, *regardless of the circumstances.*

PEACE: This is *not* a quality that requires tranquil, undisturbed surroundings. This is a *quiet, inner confidence* that is able to remain *serene and undaunted,* even when surrounded by the most chaotic or distressing circumstances.

PATIENCE: This inner trait behaves in complete contrast to the way the outer man wants to behave. The outer man tends to be short-tempered, irritable, restless, and intolerant of others' shortcomings. Patience, however, is *not easily angered.* It is willing to support the weak and *to wait as long as is necessary for someone to change.*

KINDNESS: This indicates someone with a *tender, compliant, willing heart.* A kind person *readily adapts and adjusts himself to meet another's needs.*

GOODNESS: This word portrays what we would call *a generous giver.* It is someone who is big-hearted — he lavishly distributes the "goods" that he has to those who are less fortunate.

FAITHFULNESS: Rather than being lazy, undependable, or irresponsible, a faithful person is *trustworthy, dedicated, reliable, and constant.* No matter what kind of unsettling situation is thrown at him, he does not change.

GENTLENESS: This refers to someone who is very *discerning and sensitive* to the needs of others. The quality of gentleness demonstrates itself in *compassion, empathy, tact, courtesy, and fairness.*

A person who walks in these character traits is someone against whom no one can bring a charge, no matter how hard he or she searches for one.

When Principle and Love Meet

Now let's take a deeper look at *self-control.* Here is a good working definition of this word — a definition that will effectively govern one's operating system in this life: *Self-control is living in the highest regard*

and respect for my inner man (and the ethical principles that guide him), while demonstrating love to those around me.

Each of us should continually evaluate our actions, thoughts, and words on the basis of this definition, asking ourselves, *"Is my conscience pleased with the way I am thinking about this situation? How will my behavior or words affect others?"*

The life challenges that most of us face are not precipitated by the renegade thoughts that race through our minds like shooting stars; all of us deal with those kinds of thoughts at times. On the contrary, the pivotal thoughts that must be evaluated are those that are allowed to *remain* in our minds — the meditations of our hearts that will eventually become a part of our very natures, governing our words, behaviors, and responses to the world around us.

The second question mentioned above is one that people don't really think about a great deal. *How will my behavior or words affect others?* Most of us do not have the foresight to consider how our words or actions will affect another person. We don't weigh out a situation before we act or evaluate what our decisions will mean to those around us.

But this evaluation process is absolutely critical to walking in character. Why? Because we will be continually pressured to disqualify ourselves and say, "I give up — I can't conquer this." *But it is our responsibility to make sure that never happens.*

Before we can walk confidently in the virtuous traits we've discussed, we will have to conquer *ourselves*. We must remember that **whatever we refuse to conquer will ultimately conquer us.**

So what do we do when we face a situation in which the circumstances are working overtime to convince us to disqualify ourselves? What do

we do when we face overwhelming opposition, and we are tempted to say, "I can't take this anymore! This is just too much"?

We must go back to our working definition of self-control, making sure that we are not breaking principle, and that we are loving others. We must begin to reevaluate ourselves, examining our thoughts, words, and deeds.

If we can't find anything we've personally done or said that would disqualify us from attaining the desired outcome in that situation, we can trust that the opposing circumstances did not originate from any bad seeds we have sown; rather, they have come against us to block us from attaining the prize on the other side of the mountain. And since we know there will be no prize if we do not keep blasting through that mountain, we just keep blasting away, pursuing excellence with everything that is within us, and refusing to disqualify ourselves from the destiny we are pursuing.

So how long are we willing to control ourselves? How long are we willing to be self-correctors? What are we holding on to that is worth the loss of the prize set before us? These are the questions we must all ask ourselves.

Closer Examination

It would be beneficial for each of us to take an honest look on the inside and deal with those issues that are building faulty foundations in our lives, instead of making everyone else pay the price for that which we refuse to confront. We are responsible to establish our own set of standards. If we will *choose* to deal with our own character issues, someone else will be spared the unpleasant assignment of having to do it.

A person may say, "Yes, but you just don't know my situation. You

don't know what they've done to me and what I've had to go through."

Let me share something from personal experience — the day we learn that ours is not the only perspective that matters is the day we will be free. That will be the day our passions no longer control us. Instead, our highest desire will be to embrace wise instruction and walk in integrity.

Why is this true? Because instead of torturing others by imposing our selfish outbursts upon them, we will deal with our own emotions. We will get to the point where we'll say, "That's it — I'm giving this up! I don't want this in my life anymore, so I'm taking responsibility."

We must not get into wrestling matches with others over the areas we, ourselves, need to change. We must wrestle with our own shortcomings and weaknesses, so no one else has to deal with us. Then, when we are finished, the only fruit that people will see growing on our "branches" will be love, joy, peace, patience, gentleness, kindness, goodness, faithfulness, and self-control!

Actions Breed Consequences

Self-control begins by recognizing that there is a consequence for every action. Of course, we live in a society, today, where consequences for a lack of self-control are few and far between. But we need to realize that, even though society hands out very few consequences for wrong behavior, the Universal Law of Sowing and Reaping never expires.

We may not want to hear about consequences in this day and age, but the truth still stands — if we let our selfish passions have their way, it will only be a matter of time before negative consequences begin to manifest.

Tears of sorrow can never wash away the consequence for wrongdo-

ing. Crying and wishing things were different doesn't change a person's life. Changing one's *character* changes one's life.

The proof of authenticity is the willingness to be examined. An individual of character will welcome the opportunity to have his authenticity validated. Just as the integrity of any metal is tested by fire and pressure, the integrity of a person's character is tested and tried by the fire of adversity. The gleaming gold of a person's nature cannot truly shine until the intense heat of affliction has eliminated the dross in his life.

Self-control begins when we expose our thoughts and feelings to the guidelines of proven principles, before we ever put them out in front of others. Then, once the true nature of those thoughts and emotions has been revealed, we have to choose whether or not we want to unload them on the people around us.

Choose Wisdom

It becomes so much easier to exert self-control after spending time in the light of wise instruction. After all, when wisdom and truth are readily available to us, why would we want to sacrifice precious time, or jeopardize important relationships, just so we can spend a few hours, days, or weeks feeding our selfish passions? Wouldn't we rather expose our bad attitudes to the proven wisdom of the ages? Wouldn't we rather let wisdom, love, integrity, and virtue correct those attitudes before we ever unload them on other people? Wisdom gives us the answers before the test ever comes!

So let's make the decision to establish the pillar of self-control. Let's begin to sow the right seed, as we expose every thought and emotion to the light of wisdom and truth.

We have the opportunity to decide, once and for all, that our days of failure are over; that we will no longer quit right before our victory comes; and that we have had enough of complacency and mediocrity. From now on, we are operating as a bountiful tree whose branches abundantly produce the fruit of sweet character. That's the way we're going to start every day, and that's the way we are going to *keep* every day victorious!

LIFE LESSON

One employer said to his aspiring novelist, "Progress is a matter of self-discipline."

The employee didn't understand. "C'mon," he said, "self-discipline is important for athletes and soldiers, but the only thing writers need is a good idea."

The boss smiled at the aspiring writer's oversight. "How many times, while you were trying to come up with a story, did you check your email? How long were you on the phone? How many times did you wander away from your desk to get a snack? Is it any wonder you haven't come up with a good storyline?"

The writer saw what his boss meant. So, to get the job, he spent weeks writing and perfecting his application short-stories, hardly leaving his chair except to satisfy his hunger or go to the restroom. He produced a number of highly acclaimed stories in his first months on the job; after that, however, he seemed to forget the effort it took to get him there. His boss was gracious enough to correct him gently. The writer then realized he'd better adjust his habits, or he would be released to waste his own time.

What followed was remarkable. He didn't produce any masterpieces for a number of years, but he did notice every irrelevant thing that fought for his attention. By refusing to give in to his every whim, he refined his character so much that, in the following years, he was able to write nationally recognized stories, which brought substantial income to himself and his employer. Discipline was his ticket to promotion; because of it, he became famous for his work.[1]

Don't Bite The Hand That Feeds You

Pillar 2: Compliance

"Every human being, of whatever origin, of whatever station, deserves respect. We must each respect others even as we respect ourselves."

- Ulysses S. Grant

Once an individual decides to walk in integrity, some things automatically become non-negotiable. After *sincerely committing* to a life of virtue and excellence, there's no going back to a life of compromise and mediocrity. A person can't just, one day, decide "I don't want to be part of this character stuff anymore." It is like riding on a roller coaster after it has been released from its starting point — we can't just suddenly decide that we want to get off!

Once we surrender to living by right ethics, life begins to reveal the great advantages and benefits available to us, and we discover the wonderful things we are able to accomplish. But somewhere along the way, we must reach the point where we say, "Hey, wait a second! I shouldn't just be looking for *what I can get* out of life. I must now begin looking for *what I can give back* that could benefit the lives of others."

It is at this point that we begin to learn about one of those "non-negotiables" in our journey toward character — the issue of *respect.* This is a crucial pillar. It is also the one area of our character that needs more attention than any other, for if we will readily walk in respect, then all the rest of the character traits will be easier for us to achieve.

The inner struggle of disrespect is a life-long issue for many people. Wherever we find disrespect, we will also find:

- Self-centered willfulness
- Rebellion
- Selfishness

Sadly, a great many of us, both young and old, fit this description. A person can be eighty years old and still be an all-around self-willed and insubordinate individual.

Choose Respect

Respect means *to adhere to the instructions of those in the place of decision-making; to defer, regard, honor, and esteem.* It also means *to perform what is required while abstaining from what is prohibited.*

Have you ever examined how long you mentally listen to the barrage of disrespectful thoughts, inner lies, and negative "self-talk" before you finally act upon it? How long do you withstand the pressure before you actually listen? We must eliminate the negative influences from our lives, or they will ultimately lead us down a path that none of us want to tread. **The refusal to conquer negativity ensures that it will ultimately become our master.**

A synonym for the word *respect* is "regard." To regard means *to consider or think of in a special way.* It also means *to heed and pay attention to; to diligently discern;* and *to perceive with one's ear.*

A person who has determined to be respectful, in all areas of life, does not have to have his own way. He listens; he hears; and he is *content* to follow through with the instructions he receives.

What Respect *Is Not*

Often we can find out what something *is* by learning what it *is not.* So let's learn more about respect by taking a look at its opposite.

Opposite to people who are respectful are those who are *insubordi-*

nate, *rebellious*, and *contrary*. *Willful* and *headstrong*, these individuals unyieldingly insist on achieving their own agendas. Beware...they will do all they can to wear you down, as they pressure you to see things their way.

Disrespectful, noncompliant individuals are recalcitrant, which means *stubbornly obstinate.* Once they dig their heels in the ground, we might as well build a monument around them, because they aren't moving! All these negative traits add up to men and women who are *ungovernable, ungrateful,* and *unruly*—a continual grief to those who, unfortunately, are called upon to lead them.

One can't help but be struck by the severity of this repulsive terminology: *insubordinate; rebellious; contrary; willful; headstrong; recalcitrant; ungovernable; ungrateful; unruly.* It is quite evident that **it is a person's *pride* that will inevitably demote him in life; but a humble attitude will always result in a great future.**

In studying this subject, I've come to realize that in the realm of respect or disrespect, there is no middle ground. If a person desires to have a future that is wide open, with many opportunities, there is no "right time" for him to exercise disrespect by saying, "Well, that's your opinion. I'm going to do things my way."

Nevertheless, that is exactly the way modern society wants it. These elements of disrespect, noncompliance, and pride have ushered in very dangerous and uncertain times. We live in a world where people love their own opinions. They are primarily interested in what they can get for themselves, not in what they can give to someone else.

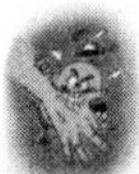

The High Cost of Honor

Today's society has paid a heavy price for this scarcity of honor and respect. What was called a dysfunctional family twenty years ago is now called a normal family. In fact, if a child has two parents living at home with him, his family is now statistically considered abnormal!

Our culture desperately needs people of character to be an answer to the lack of honor we see around us. Honor plays a pivotal role in the important arena of respect — honor for the elderly, honor for wisdom, honor for the decision-makers in life. Honor adds value to the giver as well as to the recipient.

In our modern society, slander, betrayal, and deception are unbridled and running rampant. For instance, someone might think, "I made a mistake in getting married, so I'll just change marriage partners." Or he might reason, "I made too much of a financial commitment, so I'm going to file bankruptcy."

This mentality of betrayal and compromise is common *whenever a person's foundation of character is inadequate to deal with his circumstances.*

People of character continually check to ensure that their foundation of ethics always exceeds their temptations to compromise. Whenever our ethics cannot withstand our temptations, we're in greater trouble than we understand, for our character defines who we are, both to ourselves and to those who have chosen to be around us.

Now, it isn't our fault that society has adopted a lifestyle that embraces a lack of character. It only becomes our fault when we become part of the problem. How, then, do we become part of the answer? By celebrating character, not only in our own lives but also in the lives of others.

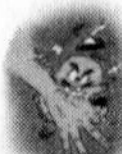

Two Philosophies

This is where it begins to get sticky. We are now facing, in our collective societies, those who, through various levels of deception and chicanery, have achieved a place of leadership that gives them a platform from which they are able to exploit the innocent. This becomes an almost insurmountable challenge because rather than seeing these positions (in government, business, marriage, parents, friends, or life) as those that are set in place to protect us, we seem to be suspicious of them all. The dishonest and insincere become the standard from which we gather our information.

After seeing, reading, and hearing of all the exploitations going on in the world, we are almost afraid to trust *ancient wisdom.* Yet, these established, enduring truths are the qualities that history is written about; they are the reasons why the greats have become great.

Therefore, regardless of our possible reticence in trusting these time-honored precepts, let us begin. Those who will dare to take a step have a great journey ahead. But those who are still afraid can always find a reason not to posture themselves in this manner; many won't believe the safeguarding power of these truths, even after repeatedly witnessing the undeniable and proven success they bring to the lives of the honorable.

People of character desire to shape and discipline their lives according to time-tested principles. Interestingly, in this day and age, many *claim* to have an interest in truth. But although the arrival of the Internet has brought an information explosion into every home, few seem to be willing to reach for and grasp *real truth.*

For every truth we discover, we will also face a counterfeit philosophy. We see this demonstrated within this issue of compliance. There are two

philosophies of compliance in the world. The following mental picture will give us an idea of these two ways of thinking.

Three men are standing on the deck of an aircraft carrier. The Sergeant in Arms, who is standing on a platform just above the deck, suddenly cries out, "Take cover! Hit the deck!"

Two of the men immediately hit the deck. The third man remains standing, asking, "Why? What's happening?" In an instant, a missile explodes on the deck. The men who took cover survive the blast, but shrapnel kills the third man, who failed to heed the Sergeant's warning.

The third man demonstrated an understanding of compliance that is built upon counterfeit philosophy. He remained standing on the deck, asking the question, "Why?" *Only when he understood the reason behind the command was he willing to comply.*

Modern Western culture bases its understanding of compliance upon this philosophy. In this age of independence and information gathering, a person asks questions first and *then* decides if he wants to obey.

In the past, when greater respect for authority and leadership was demonstrated, people usually didn't have to be asked a second time to do anything. They complied the first time, without questioning, because they not only believed in the integrity of the person who had given them the instruction, but they also possessed an internal trait of trust.

This is a more ancient and accurate understanding of compliance. It tells us that a person *complies first* and seeks to understand later. Any questions he then asks are not to test the one who gave the instruction, but to preemptively prepare for wise decision-making in the future. **Character proves its respect for virtue through its compliance to moral precepts.**

If we choose to live according to the counterfeit philosophy of compliance, the day will come when we will wish we had learned to instantly comply. A leader will say, "Take cover!" and while we are standing there, insisting on knowing why, a "missile" will hit us from behind, bringing destruction and loss.

Secrets to Living a Life of Compliance

There are two secrets to living a compliant life. First, *we are to love truth.* Every choice to obey, in this life, is based on our love for integrity and truth, for that love transcends everything. It is the reason we can stay in difficult situations or continue to deal with difficult people. **Ethical character bases all of life on the all-encompassing love for truth.**

Our highest priority must be to search for truth, for that is what will motivate us toward a life of compliance. Because of our love for truth, we will be willing to work through challenges and maintain what is right.

Here is the second secret to living a compliant life: *We are to always keep the principles and precepts of truth*. That word "keep" means *to guard, to protect, and to defend.* Above all else, one must guard his heart, for what a man believes in his heart affects everything he does.

Accuracy must be continually pursued, in order to protect truth. We can't be careless or half-hearted in our pursuit. We can't be double-minded, saying, "I love truth, but I'm going to exaggerate it a little bit, to my advantage," or "I am a man of virtue, but I'm going to get back at that person for what he did to me!" A person of integrity does not assume that, at his own whims, he can stop guarding his commitment to truth.

Compliance doesn't have at its destination merely the pleasing of others. It is the choice we make in order to achieve the life we were designed to live. **Compliance is not merely a recommendation; it is a *requirement* of true success.** It isn't an option in the lives of men and women who carry virtue at their core.

The simple fact, concerning all wise instruction, is that we will garner benefits if we choose to comply and suffer loss if we don't. If we choose willingness and compliance, we will experience the good things that life has to offer — health, freedom, rich and fulfilling relationships, and prosperity of mind, soul, and body.

But if we refuse compliance and rebel against the wisdom of ethical principles, we will be destroyed by our enemies, whether they are greed, disease, toxic relationships, or poverty.

Guaranteed Destruction

There isn't a great deal of wiggle room in these matters. Even if others act wrongfully toward us, we must remain unchanged, because we know this is what principle requires of us. On the other hand, if we choose to walk the road of resistance, we better squeeze out all the "enjoyment" we can, knowing that destruction will get the last laugh in our lives!

Noncompliance is one of the most personally destructive things we could ever deal with in life. We have probably all encountered a difficult and noncompliant person at one time or another. We can talk to him until we're blue in the face, but "Mr. Noncompliant" will never heed wise warnings or make the changes that are necessary to vacate that most certain path of destruction.

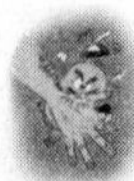

What we often miss, when we are feeling defiant, is that our noncompliance and self-willed attitudes not only affect others, but, worse than that, *they really hurt us.* We might not like the person to whom we should comply, but the consequences of noncompliance are far worse than submitting to the requests of those we "dislike" in life! We must discipline ourselves to live and respond according to ethics, not according to feelings.

There are many who have destroyed their own lives due to their failure to espouse ethics. Initially, these individuals may have applied wisdom. They might have even experienced a level of improvement. But, eventually, they started to listen to the voice of compromise—the voice that says, "You don't need integrity and truth anymore. You don't need to be bound by the discipline of these principles." In time, they allowed their personal standards to fade and, ultimately, they let go of "truth" in their hearts. The moment they did, was the moment they started to fail, often blaming others for their demise!

Where does that kind of behavior come from? It arises from an ignorance concerning consequences. We need to be willing to embrace this fact about life: **Just because we may not see any *immediate* negative outcomes from our poor choices doesn't mean we can put compliance off to the side and never suffer the consequences.** As long as we choose to walk in noncompliance, we will not enjoy the fulfillment and peace that compliance has to offer.

Life resists the man who is proud and arrogant, but it gives abundant opportunities to the person who is willing to comply with the leadership structures in life. **Integrity is withheld from anyone who refuses to possess a spirit of compliance.**

Examining Ourselves

The following questions are helpful in shining the light of truth into the crevices of our hearts, as we seek to determine whether or not we are compliant individuals:

1. Do we act on what has been requested of us?

Remember, compliance is based on ethics and truth. It is not based on the way *we* think we should do something.

Let this dispel any confusion: Unquestioning compliance is not the same as blind obedience. A person must never give up his personal responsibility to understand truth for himself and then do whatever he believes is right.

2. Do we ask for reasons why, when our requests are denied?

Asking questions to learn or to clarify information is commendable and even, in fact, advisable; but having a *questioning attitude* is not. When a person requests something, and that request is denied, does he insist on knowing why? If so, he is flirting with noncompliance.

3. Do we respond immediately when given a request?

Or do we say, "I'll get to it when I can"? Compliance means stopping what *we* want to do, in order to fulfill the desire of the person we are there to please.

4. Do we grudgingly respond to instruction?

Do we respond to instructions with a smile, or do we look like we're dealing with an upset stomach? Compliance doesn't just mean grudgingly doing what we're asked to do; it means *cheerfully* responding to a

request, whether or not we understand the reason behind the request. Compliance is doing the job now and understanding later.

5. *Do we ever give excuses for why we cannot fulfill a request?*

"Excusiologists" always seem to have encyclopedias filled with reasons for noncompliance. Conversely, the compliant continually search for ways to overcome obstacles.

6. *Do we frequently have to be reminded to do something we were asked to do?*

Compliance doesn't put off an assigned task, according to the whims of its own convenience.

7. *Do we often have to redo assignments, because we do them incorrectly or with mediocrity?*

Compliance is being diligent to correctly follow instructions the first time. Remember: *Instructions repeated become correction...*

Finally, this principle reveals the ultimate test of compliance: *Are we carrying out every word and deed according to <u>our own desires</u> or the desires of the one who has made the request?*

Honoring Others

A person of noncompliance is someone who continually disregards the instructions that are given to him. He might be a nice person, but when asked for something, he just doesn't seem to find the time to get around to it. When we do that, we are actually showing a disregard for honor and ethics. We are forgetting that every thought, word, and action is a planted seed that will produce a harvest sometime in the future.

Suppose our previously discussed corporate executive asks one of his staff members to pick up some office supplies. The next day comes and, as soon as the employee is asked, he says, "Oh, I forgot, but I'll get them tomorrow."

The next morning, as the executive leaves the office to attend a meeting, he says to his subordinate, "Okay, now remember to pick up the supplies." But when he returns to the office that evening, he is told, "Oh, I forgot again." At that point, the employee is no longer just forgetful; he is disregarding a request, which is actually passive rebellion.

We can't operate in this manner if we want to be significant in this world. The Law of Sowing and Reaping is very precise. We may have several positive character traits, but rarely do those override the negative ones. As an old saying goes, "Putting confidence in an unreliable person is like chewing with a toothache or walking on a broken foot."

Always keep in mind that **leaders aren't looking to measure our maturity; their eyes are fixed on our compliance.**

No Substitute

Before I was ever in a position of leadership, I taught a study group that was growing and quite successful. One evening, an individual attended the group and later went to my supervisor, reporting that I had taught something that he believed was wrong.

A few days later, my supervisor's secretary told me that he wanted to see me in his office.

When I met him in his office that evening, he said to me, "I bet you wonder why I called you here today."

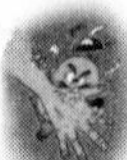

I replied, "No, sir. I'm convinced the reason you called me here is that you want to give me some type of promotion."

He replied, "Wrong. Actually, I have a mind to bench you and make sure you never stand in an instructor's position again."

I stopped him there and said, "Excuse me, sir. Please forgive me for interrupting, but if you tell me to never teach again for the rest of my life, I will never again stand up in front of a group of people."

At that, the man became silent. He couldn't think of an answer, so the conversation ended. But for years afterward, he did everything he could possibly do to discredit me.

I asked him, "What are you going to do with the study group? I will gladly give it back to you."

He said, "You can take it."

I replied, "I'm not taking anything. The study group is not mine to take. But, if you'd like to give it back to me, that is another thing."

Then, the man said, "Oh, go ahead and take it. I don't care what happens to it. It can die, for all I care."

In my own heart, I had no choice but to keep teaching that group; they were so hungry for instruction. Nevertheless, it was extremely difficult. After all, the same man who had once supported me became the one who was discrediting me! I determined not to let the group die. It grew and grew, and became what is now an international organization that trains and equips leaders.

Many factors were involved in the growth of this organization, but the fact remains: **There is absolutely no substitute for a soft and compliant heart.**

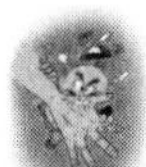

Life Lesson

As a high school coach, I did all I could to help my boys win their games. I rooted as hard for victory as they did. A dramatic incident, however, following a game in which I officiated as a referee, changed my perspective on victories and defeats.

I was refereeing a league championship basketball game in New Rochelle, New York, between New Rochelle and Yonkers High. Dan O'Brien was coaching the New Rochelle team, and the Yonkers coach was Les Beck. The gym was crowded to capacity, and the volume of noise made it impossible to hear. The game was well played and closely contested. Yonkers was leading by one point, as I glanced at the clock and discovered there was but 30 seconds left to play.

Yonkers, in possession of the ball, passed off, shot, and missed. New Rochelle recovered, pushed the ball up the court, and shot. The ball rolled tantalizingly around the rim and dropped off. The fans shrieked. New Rochelle, the home team, recovered the ball and tapped it in for what looked like a victory. The tumult was deafening. I glanced at the clock and saw that the game was over. I checked with the other official, but he could not help me.

Still seeking help in this bedlam, I approached the timekeeper, a young man of 17 years old or so. He said, "Mr. Covino, the buzzer went off as the ball rolled off the rim, before the final tap-in was made."

I was in the unbelievable position of having to tell Coach O'Brien the sad news. "Dan," I said, "time ran out before the final basket was tapped in. Yonkers won the game."

His face clouded over. The young timekeeper came up to us. He said, "I'm sorry, DAD. The time ran out before the final basket."

Suddenly, like the sun coming out from behind a cloud, Coach O'Brien's face lit up. He said, "That's okay, Joe. You did what you had to do. I'm proud of you." Turning to me, he said, "Al, I want you to meet my son, Joe."

The two of them walked off the court together, the coach's arm around his son's shoulder.[1]

On The Level

Pillar 3: Honesty

"I hope I shall always possess firmness and virtue enough to maintain what I consider the most enviable of all titles, the character of an 'Honest Man.'"

- George Washington

As we've all likely discovered by now, we can't expect our face-to-face encounter with our own poor character to be a simple "walk in the park." It is very possible that, at this point, each of us may be thinking, *"The person who has been the most deceived about my character is me."*

This self-deception is pervasive in our society because toxic, blame-shifting "victimitis" permeates the very air we breathe. People are inventing new ways to spin and twist a lie in almost every area of life. They do this, in part, because they don't believe they can bear the pain or pay the price for being honest. What is possibly the worst reason of all, is that they may do it because they won't even tell *themselves* the truth.

A simple definition of honesty is this: *behavior, in words and actions, that aims to convey the truth.* Conversely, dishonesty is *a manner of speaking or acting that causes people to be misled or deluded.* This deception continues until they are cheated out of something that belongs to them in the relationship.

A person who fails to tell *himself* the truth is, in reality, a dishonest person. He may speak words that seem very kind. But, he is actually more interested in convincing others, concerning his kindness, than he is in eliminating the lies that he perpetually tells himself.

So, to discover a person's true identity and motive, we can't just read his résumé — we have to watch what he *does*. We must always listen with our *eyes*, not with our *ears*, for our eyes will tell us much more than

our ears ever could. We must remember that **a person who possesses genuine character aligns his life with the words of his mouth.**

One who plays both sides of the fence is a dishonest person — self-preserving on one side, while pretending to buy into everything you're saying on the other. Watch out for a person like this, because this kind of ambivalent behavior is only the beginning.

Eventually, this person will cheat people out of the mutual benefits that a relationship with him should generate. As he fails to produce a harvest from the seed others have planted in his life, he will begin to cover up the truth of his situation — not only from other people but from himself as well.

A person might try to squirm out of this sobering thought by saying, "Well, you know, I don't really lie. I just don't tell the whole, complete truth."

A person who tells half-truths doesn't really believe that he lies. He thinks that if he tells half the truth, he is not deceiving others. However, there is a big problem with that way of thinking, for it will not only keep that individual from ever walking fully in the truth, but it will also bring destruction and heartache into his surroundings.

Many people who believe themselves to be honest individuals are far too nonchalant about telling half-truths. Here is a common excuse they often use: "Well, you know what I meant — you know what's in my heart." Yes, we may know what this person meant. But if we really want to know what is in his heart, we need to watch and see if his actions line up with the words of his mouth.

We don't really even know our *own* hearts, until we start speaking, and then watch to see if our actions are consistent with our words and intentions!

Dishonest Roots

We fail to tell ourselves the truth for one of three reasons:

1. *We don't tell ourselves the truth because of an OVER-inflated idea about ourselves and our contributions in any set of circumstances.*

   This form of pride causes us to think more highly of ourselves than we ought to think.

2. *We don't tell ourselves the truth because of an UNDER-inflated opinion of ourselves.*

   This is more commonly known as low self-esteem.

One form of pride makes us believe that we are better than we are; the other form makes us believe that we are not good enough for anything. Both are *pride*, because they cause us to focus on ourselves rather than on others. Both forms of pride are lies that keep us from being honest with ourselves.

3. *We don't tell ourselves the truth because of ignorance.*

Ignorance is simply a lack of knowledge. Sound innocent enough? Try again; people are *destroyed* for lack of knowledge!

There are actually two categories of ignorance. First, a person is ignorant of an issue when *he doesn't know about it or isn't aware of it.*

Although there may be some who are ignorant because they simply don't know, most people are not always as lacking in knowledge as they pretend to be. The great majority of them fit into the second category of ignorance: *Those who know the truth but ignore it.*

There's an old saying that goes something like this: "Deception wouldn't be so deceptive if it wasn't so deceiving!" It sounds so obvious

as to be silly; yet, millions live their whole lives in self-deception. On the outside, they act very positive and strong in their commitment to integrity. But on the inside, they have a weak, negative nature that they won't admit to, even to themselves. They don't tell themselves the truth and, therefore, they live and die inside of a lie. These people might be all bubbly and positive on the outside, but are they truly successful on the inside?

The real trap is that no one can tell just one lie. That lie becomes the "mother lie" that suddenly begins to breed one new lie after another. Why? Because the person has to keep telling another lie to make the last one seem believable! Soon, he is tangled in the sticky web of his own deceit. As Sir Walter Scott once said, "Oh, what a tangled web we weave, when first we practice to deceive!"

Conversely, what does character do? **Right character seeks to root out every hidden lie that keeps one living in defeat.** It is up to each of us to make sure we don't live inside our own self-made house of lies. To that end, we need to take the time to honestly evaluate whether or not we are telling ourselves the truth, in every area of life. For instance, are we unapproachable about certain issues? Have we failed to allow our hearts to be touched by the seriousness of our need for change?

Honesty Hurts

Ethics require that we are honest not only with ourselves but also with others, especially when confrontation is needed. **An individual who esteems the pillar of honesty is willing to speak the truth in love, even if it may hurt.**

Occasionally, it becomes necessary to talk to someone who just doesn't seem to understand the severity of his own situation. If he doesn't recognize

the potential consequences of his wrong behavior, someone must confront that person with the truth. Remember, the "wounds" of a true friend will bring healing, change, and beneficial growth.

"But my friend just doesn't want to talk about the areas he needs to change."

Well then, that person isn't a true friend.

"Yes, but I don't have many friends, so I really want to work with this person."

Those who insist on pursuing a lack of character do not qualify to be our friends if we value virtue and integrity as essential foundations of life. We would have to lower our standards in order to keep that particular "friend."

How important is it to speak the truth at *all* times, even when it is painful? Consider the following hypothetical situation.

Let's say that a guy named Bill (an honest guy who has already made 99 truthful statements this particular day) is being held hostage by a thief, who is hiding behind Bill's front door with a loaded gun.

Bill's friend, Tom, walks into the room and says: "I heard a news report about an escaped convict in the area — they say he's armed and dangerous. Have you seen anybody suspicious hangin' around?"

Bill replies, "No."

The next thing you know, the thief steps out from behind the door and shoots Tom, who falls down dead.

Admittedly, Bill had already told 99 truths that day; and *he only told one lie.* Yet, what was the key factor that led to Bill's friend being shot? Did Tom benefit from Bill's previous truthfulness? Or did he lose his life over Bill's one lie?

People don't understand how important this principle is. They want to spend all their time telling their friends how great they are, instead of loving them enough to tell them the truth. They need to hear the truth, even if it hurts. Remember — the *wounds* of a friend will ultimately bring healing to them.

Contrary to what many believe, a person is actually a *faithful* friend when he confronts someone with the truth about shortcomings that are keeping him from being successful. If a friend does something that is offensive or unethical, we must go to them and speak to them about it. Rather than talking *about* them or storming out of their life, a true friend will *speak the truth, no matter what the cost!*

Many individuals just can't figure out why they are having a difficult time in their lives. There is often one primary reason — they are not telling the truth to themselves or others. However, **character lives a life of truth and sincerity before all men.**

The fact is, we are never going to get anywhere if we are not willing to first confront ourselves with the truth, and then make those around us aware of when we have lied. It is imperative that we are honest before all men, including ourselves.

The truth is that **the only person who cannot see a blind spot is the one who has it.** This is the reason that influencers are sent to us in life — to help us recognize those areas of needed change that we cannot or *will not* see on our own. We must welcome and celebrate the people who fill that all-so-important role in our lives; otherwise, we will hit impasses where we can advance no further in pursuing our dreams.

Each of us needs to have at least one person, in life, whom we trust and esteem to that extent. If this person tells us we have a blind spot

that's tripping us up, we shouldn't even ask a question. We should accept that it's true and immediately begin to work on ourselves.

Sadly, if we are like most people, we don't have this kind of trusted friend in our lives. If we trust only ourselves, we are very susceptible to living lives of self-deception.

How do we react toward our friends when they are straight up with us? Do they now become our enemies because they've told us the truth? Would we rather believe a flatterer's "sweet lies," instead of accepting the uncomfortable truth from a friend?

This particular principle boils down to one thing: *Being willing to trust.* We must trust that we can give our lives over to the truth; and we must trust those people in our lives who will speak the truth to us when we need it the most.

Integrity Wanted: Apply Inside

We can discern a lot by watching people and observing how they react when the issue of integrity is brought up. When we talk to an honest person about honesty, it doesn't bother him. In fact, it makes him happy, because he is committed to personal improvement. Only a dishonest person gets upset when the subject of honesty comes up.

It is not always easy to tell if someone is walking in honesty and integrity. People can, and will, attempt to run and hide; but just give it enough time, and the lies (or the truths) that live inside a person *will* eventually become clear.

This subject of integrity is crucial to the survival of our societies, our families, and our individual aspirations. We are not going to advance in

life as long as we remain dishonest with ourselves and with others. Without honesty, everything that has been given to us will fall through the gaping cracks of self-deception.

This is true for every one of us. We all have to come to a place in our lives where we say, "I refuse to let deception rule my life any longer!"

It's very exciting when a person decides to stop hiding; he is suddenly *set free from himself.* He finally quits trying to make others think that he's somebody he's not. Only then does he find out that he truly *is* somebody!

Think about all the valuable tools that have been provided to help us walk in truth. We have ethical principles and precepts to teach us, as well as willing mentors to guide us. We have the examples of great men and women who have lived their lives in truth and integrity. We have no excuse for living without honesty and transparency in our relationships. It's time to embrace truthfulness in every aspect of our lives — before others and, most certainly, before ourselves!

Life Lesson

Once there was an emperor, in the Far East, who was growing old and knew it was coming time to choose his successor. Instead of choosing one of his assistants or one of his own children, he decided to do something different.

He called all the young people in the kingdom together one day. He said, "It has come time for me to step down and to choose the next emperor. I have decided to choose one of you." The kids were shocked! But the emperor continued. "I am going to give each one of you a seed today.

One seed. It is a very special seed. I want you to go home, plant the seed, water it, and come back here, one year from today, with what you have grown from this one seed. I will then judge the plants that you bring to me, and the one I choose will be the next emperor of the kingdom!"

There was one boy, named Ling, who was there that day, and he, like the others, received a seed. He went home and excitedly told his mother the whole story. She helped him get a pot and some planting soil, and he planted the seed and watered it carefully. Every day, he would water it and watch to see if it had grown.

After about three weeks, some of the other youths began to talk about their seeds and the plants that were beginning to grow. Ling kept going home and checking his seed, but nothing ever grew. Three weeks, four weeks, five weeks went by. Still nothing.

By now, others were talking about their plants. But Ling didn't have a plant, and he felt like a failure. Six months went by, and there was still nothing in Ling's pot. He just knew he had killed his seed. Everyone else had trees and tall plants, but he had nothing. Ling didn't say anything to his friends, however. He just kept waiting for his seed to grow.

A year finally went by, and all the youths of the kingdom brought their plants to the emperor for inspection. Ling told his mother that he wasn't going to take an empty pot. But she encouraged him to go, to take his pot, and to be honest about what had happened. Ling felt sick to his stomach, but he knew his mother was right. He took his empty pot to the palace.

When Ling arrived, he was amazed at the variety of plants grown by all the other youths. They were beautiful, in all shapes and sizes. Ling put his empty pot on the floor, and many of the other kids laughed at him. A

few felt sorry for him and just said, "Hey, nice try."

When the emperor arrived, he surveyed the room and greeted the young people. Ling just tried to hide in the back. "My, what great plants, trees, and flowers you have grown," said the emperor. "Today, one of you will be appointed the next emperor!"

All of a sudden, the emperor spotted Ling at the back of the room with his empty pot. He ordered his guards to bring him to the front. Ling was terrified. "The emperor knows I'm a failure! Maybe he will have me killed!"

When Ling got to the front, the emperor asked his name. "My name is Ling," he replied. All the kids were laughing and making fun of him.

The emperor asked everyone to quiet down. He looked at Ling and then announced to the crowd, "Behold your new emperor! His name is Ling!" Ling couldn't believe it. He couldn't even grow his seed. How could he be the new emperor?

Then the emperor said, "One year ago today, I gave everyone here a seed. I told you to take the seed, plant it, water it, and bring it back to me today. But I gave you all boiled seeds, which would not grow. All of you, except Ling, have brought me trees and plants and flowers. When you found that the seed would not grow, you substituted another seed for the one I gave you. Ling was the only one with the courage and honesty to bring me a pot with my seed in it. Therefore, he is the one who will be the new emperor!"[1]

WE APPRECIATE THE HONESTY OF YOUR PERSONAL ASSESSMENT, SIR, BUT THE SIGN INDICATES THE DEPTH OF THE WATER, NOT YOUR CHARACTER
SHALLOW
VILEY ©1995 WASHINGTON POST WRITERS GROUP 5-27

Find It In Your Heart

Pillar 4: Compassion

"Compassion is the antitoxin of the soul: where there is compassion, even the most poisonous impulses remain relatively harmless."

- Eric Hoffer

Compassion is an absolutely vital quality for us to cultivate in life, if we want to walk in ethical character. Having ethics and integrity implies that we are actively cultivating a deep regard for the worth and dignity of human life, no matter what the hardships or circumstances.

Have you ever thought of what it means to be a compassionate person? Compassion is *an attitude of care and concern, grounded in pity and sympathy toward others.* It refers to *the ability to commiserate with another individual who is going through difficult times in life.* Other ingredients of this mighty, life-altering force include *pity, sympathy, mercy, kindness, tenderness, clemency, empathy, solicitousness, caring,* and *consideration.*

The dictionary says that compassion also includes *suffering with another person* or *painful sympathy.* Compassion actually combines both love and sorrow, for a person of compassion is willing to share in the pain that someone else is going through. Thus, compassion also refers to *a sensation of sorrow that is activated by the distress or the misfortunes of another.*

At times, a person of compassion will even feel anger, as he puts himself in the shoes of the distressed, empathizes with him, and experiences the emotional pain that his friend is feeling. This warrantable anger is actually a manifestation of deep compassion flowing from one person to another. In sharing another's pain, compassion helps to lift the heavy burden.

Some people have the idea that compassion is not a very important quality to pursue. However, they would think differently if they stood in a position of leadership, where compassion is a *must-have* attribute.

Many times, after someone has erred, he is in need of a fresh start. He acknowledges his slip-up and wants the opportunity to make it right. Only an authority figure can provide that person with the fresh start he needs. But without compassion, those who are the leaders in his life would never be interested in giving him another opportunity to prove he can do things the right way.

Compassion provides a fresh start to anyone who sincerely commits to the pursuit of change — those who are willing to:

- Admit they did wrong
- Bring forth restitution
- Embrace character and integrity as their standard for self-correction

A Tender, Selfless Heart

Compassion and tenderheartedness are integrally connected. In fact, we cannot have one quality without the other. We should, therefore, continually seek to nurture tender hearts toward others.

Although compassion covets the prize of a tender heart, people who have tender hearts are hard to find. It is a rare person who *quickly responds* to the whispered promptings of his conscience, as soon as he hears them. When relating to a tenderhearted person, one is quickly able to get past his natural reasoning and penetrate his heart with the truth; he will respond to what is right every time.

Parents can quickly see the difference between a tender and a stubborn heart, just by looking at their children. Parents will often have children who fit into both categories. One child might be strong-willed and stubborn, whereas another child might be softhearted and pliable. A child who fits the latter description is like putty in their hands. As the tenderhearted child grows, his parents will be able to form him into an extraordinary person.

Meekness Is Not Weakness

People don't mind receiving compassion from others, but they often refrain from giving it because they think it is a sign of weakness. But compassion is not weakness. It is actually a rare demonstration of *strength*, for compassion possesses an unrelenting desire for right and truth to prevail.

A compassionate person wants to right the wrongs he sees. He yearns to silence the roar from years of disappointment in the life of another. He wants to answer questions that others are unwilling to even acknowledge. He willingly takes the responsibility to become the shock absorber for other people's lives — even when he doesn't feel like doing it and even when those individuals don't deserve it. His heart's desire is to help remove the obstacles from others, so they can get in a position to get back on track and finally start succeeding. **Compassion is willing to put its shoulder under the pain of another, to momentarily lighten the load.**

The opposite of compassion is *indifference*. The attitude of an indifferent person is, "I don't care what you're going through, because I'm not the one who has to deal with it. You deal with your own pain, and I'll deal

with mine." This may sound harsh and unrealistic but, truth be known, it happens most of the time, if not in words then certainly in actions.

This is the attitude of the selfish — not of those who walk by ethical principle. However, as we establish the pillar of compassion in our lives, we will set ourselves free from the *self-centeredness* that has plagued us from our earliest memories.

When men and women of principle observe that a fellow human being is going through a difficult time, they will strive to encourage and restore their comrade. They consider and remember that, as members of the human race, they, too, are susceptible to temptation, adversity, and heartbreak; so, they desire to help bear their brother's burden.

The word "bear" means *to position oneself underneath the pain or the weight of another.* This enables that needy person to stand upright and to gain enough strength to, once again, carry his own burden of responsibility.

This individual relieves the pain of another. He erases the shame. He lifts up the weighty burden. He shares the heavy load that someone else has been enduring all alone.

We must develop a desire to live a life of uncompromised principle, for one primary purpose — *to show others how to walk out of their own personal prisons of pain*. How? By pursuing deep compassion, which is **the cloak that character wears during the moments it is relating to a dying world.**

We are to be people of compassion, kindness, humility, gentleness, and patience. It doesn't matter if we didn't learn this while growing up. We can now learn how to reject indifference and selfishness, and begin to embrace compassion, kindness, and mercy.

SOMETHING YOU *DO*, NOT JUST ACKNOWLEDGE

Compassion must be shown in our *actions*. If we see someone struggling with problems and needs, and we close our eyes and hearts to his pain, how can we claim to be caring people? **A person of character demonstrates compassion by actions, for it is hollow when expressed by words alone.**

Of course, it is important to stay alert for deceptive "con artists." These people are usually irresponsible freeloaders who wish to take advantage of those of us who are really committed to helping the needy.

Remember this: We, ourselves, will be helped *as we first seek to help others.* The Universal Law of Sowing and Reaping will always operate for our benefit, as we demonstrate genuine compassion for those around us. This law states that *whatever a man sows, he eventually reaps.*

As people of compassion, we are summoned to:

1. **Help bring truth to people who are caught in self-deception and ignorance**
2. **Help carry heavy burdens with which people are struggling**
3. **Fight for the freedom of the oppressed and the protection of the innocent**
4. **Offer the rescuing power of wisdom and truth to those who desire to escape poverty, dependency, and addiction**
5. **Share our food with the hungry**
6. **Provide hospitality to the poor and the outcasts of society**
7. **Clothe those whom we find naked**

Acts of kindness are the "get-well cards" left in the hearts of the broken by those who are compassionate. We must determine to become people of action instead of people of mere talk. Our lives consist of what

we *do*, not what we *say*. We may think we are compassionate individuals, but until we see how we respond to the tests that come our way, we will never truly know what kind of people we are. Sympathy or good intentions do nothing to bear another's burden — *actions do.*

All we need to do is stop listening to a person's words and begin *listening to their actions.* Watch how he responds to those less fortunate than himself. Check to see if he makes himself scarce when his friends are going through rough times. Ask his wife how he treats her behind closed doors. That is how we can know who a person truly is.

"I'm a man of compassion," someone might say. But what about all the insensitive, flippant responses he gives to those who are hurting? We are people of compassion not because *we* say we are but because *others* say we are. Life becomes very simple when we understand this principle.

As we express compassion to others — not only with *words* but also with *deeds* — we experience great fulfillment. Personal freedom and prosperity dawn in our lives just as predictably as the sun comes up over the eastern horizon every morning at sunrise!

What To Do

History records many examples of compassionate behavior toward the oppressed and the needy. Here are just a few of these examples.

In approximately 1520 B.C., in the Middle East, there lived an extremely wealthy man named Job. Job recorded these thoughts about his deeds of compassion to the poor and needy, before calamity hit his own life:

> Because I delivered the poor who cried out — the fatherless and the one who had no helper — the blessing of a perishing man came upon me, and I caused the widow's heart to sing for joy.
>
> My justice was like a robe and a turban. I was eyes to the blind, and I was feet to the lame. I was a father to the poor, and I searched out the case that I did not know.[1]

Bathsheba, the mother of the great King Solomon, exhorted her son to show compassion to the poor and the needy, as he carried out his duties as king of Israel. She told him to speak up for those who could not speak for themselves and to uphold the rights of all who were destitute. She told him to judge fairly and to defend the rights of the mistreated and abused.

Orphans and widows are a frequently neglected group of people on whom we are to have compassion. This would include those who come from broken homes and the elderly who live alone. We are to visit the fatherless and the widows, showing compassion toward them by finding ways to help them meet their needs.

We sometimes forget that when people grow older, they have a need for conversation with others, just as we all do. It is, therefore, important that we find time to visit the elderly and look for ways to show compassion toward them. Many of these people have no family. We need to remember to reach out to them during the holidays and other special times of the year. We can probably all find someone who doesn't have anywhere to go and invite that person to share in our holiday festivities.

When we help others, it is so important to speak to them of our own successes in conquering discouragement and defeat. People need to realize that they can come out of their present difficulties victoriously, just as we have triumphantly came out of our past trials.

King David, Solomon's father, wrote about his experiences in having compassion on those who were sick:

> But as for me, when they were sick, my clothing was sackcloth; I humbled myself with fasting; and my prayer would return to my own heart.
>
> I paced about as though he were my friend or brother; I bowed down heavily, as one who mourns for his mother.[2]

Interestingly, David was talking about his enemies! He was saying, "I wasn't out for revenge against my enemies. I was not hoping they would suffer for their wickedness against me! Instead, when my enemies were sick, I dealt with the situation as if I were the one going through the pain; and I received the compassion *I* needed, *when I showed compassion toward them."*

Several years ago, an ordinary citizen in Baltimore, Maryland was put into the kind of desperate situation that immediately exposes a man's true character. Here is his story:

> Donald Hughes was a thirty-year-old labor crew leader with Baltimore's parks and recreation department. He was the tenth child born into a lower-class family of eleven brothers and sisters. Though he had excelled as a football wide receiver in high school and had been offered several full-ride football scholarships at prestigious universities, he chose, instead, to stay home and pursue a career with the city's park department.
>
> "I've made my decision," he had told his mother one afternoon. "I want to financially help the family. It's the right thing to do."
>
> "Well, son," his mother had replied, "it's your decision. And somehow I believe your football years were not a waste. You never

know when those skills will come in handy."

One hot summer day, as Donald was doing maintenance work, he heard a commotion across the street. People were pointing to a small eighteen-month-old toddler perched on the fourth-floor window ledge of an apartment complex. There was nothing between the baby and the pavement below — at any moment he could fall to a certain death.

Donald began to quickly move toward the apartment building, knowing that his timing must be perfect. Just then, the toddler lost his balance and toppled over the edge of the window, falling toward the concrete below. Keeping his eyes on the child, Donald ran hard and fast, timing himself so that he would arrive just under the baby. He stretched out his arms, imagining that he was making a touchdown catch for the biggest game of his life. As he reached out a bit further and caught the child in his arms, the force of the weight caused him to momentarily lose his balance — but just inches before the baby hit the pavement, Donald swept him tightly into his arms.

Later that month, the mayor honored Donald for his bravery and compassion, declaring June 10th *Donald Hughes Day* in Baltimore, Maryland.[3]

Compassion is a rare find on this earth. We may find individuals who will periodically show sympathy toward the needy. Others might crusade for all kinds of humanitarian causes. However, there are very few people of *true compassion.*

Paradoxically, we find that *we* are the ones who benefit the most from our compassionate acts toward others. **If you allow compassion to flow *through* you, you will discover more compassion *within* you.** Many people have found that their own lives immensely prospered as a result of the

flow of deep compassion through their lives into the lives of others! They have discovered that character is the recipient of compassion's reward.

Compassion Doesn't Mean Compromise

As generous as we are with our compassion toward others, we must always purify our actions through the filter of principle. We want to feel what people go through, yet without compromise. We want to understand their plight and be moved internally to help them, but that does not mean we are willing to change our stance on principle.

We must always prize integrity above relationship. That is why we must not be persuaded to compromise. If we will stick with principle, we will still be on the road to success many years after those who thought they were going somewhere have fallen by the wayside. And if we determine to walk that road with genuine compassion continually flowing out of us to others, we will enjoy a life of rich and abundant reward.

The reward of compassion is ours to claim. As we continue building a strong, solid foundation of character in our lives, graciously and compassionately helping to bear the burdens of pain that others are facing, we will find our own lives improving. Because we take on the pain of others, compassion will come back to us, comforting us in our times of need and fulfilling the deepest desires of our hearts.

LIFE LESSON

A frail old man went to live with his son, daughter-in-law, and four-year-old grandson. The old man's hands trembled, his eyesight was blurred, and his step faltered. The family ate together at the table, but the elderly grandfather's shaky hands and failing sight made eating difficult. Peas rolled off his spoon onto the floor. When he grasped the glass, milk spilled on the tablecloth.

The son and daughter-in-law became irritated with the mess. "We must do something about Grandfather," said the son. "I've had enough of his spilled milk, noisy eating, and food on the floor." Therefore, the husband and wife set a small table in the corner. There, Grandfather ate alone, while the rest of the family enjoyed dinner.

Since Grandfather had broken a dish or two, his food was served in a wooden bowl. When the family glanced in Grandfather's direction, sometimes he had a tear in his eye, as he sat alone. Still, the only words the couple had for him were sharp admonitions when he dropped a fork or spilled food.

The four-year-old watched it all in silence. One evening, before supper, the father noticed his son playing with wood scraps on the floor. He asked the child sweetly, "What are you making?"

Just as sweetly, the boy responded, "Oh, I am making a little bowl for you and Mama to eat your food in, when I grow up." The four-year-old smiled and went back to work. The words so struck the parents that they were speechless. Then tears started to stream down their cheeks. Though no word was spoken, both knew what must be done.

That evening, the husband took Grandfather's hand and gently led him back to the family table. For the remainder of his days, he ate every meal with the family. And for some reason, neither husband nor wife seemed to care any longer when a fork was dropped, milk was spilled, or the tablecloth was soiled.

Children are remarkably perceptive. Their eyes ever observe, their ears ever listen, and their minds ever process the messages they absorb. If they see us patiently provide a happy home atmosphere for family members, they will imitate that attitude for the rest of their lives. The wise parent realizes that, every day, the building blocks are being laid for the child's future. Let us be wise builders and role models.

Always remember: What goes around comes around! We must treat others as we, ourselves, would like to be treated.[4]

GARFIELD, YOU LACK AMBITION...
AND PERSONALITY...
AND SELF-CONTROL, AND TACT, AND COMPASSION, AND...
WE MAY BE HERE FOR A WHILE
JIM DAVIS 3-15
www.garfield.com
Distributed by Universal Uclick
© 2010 PAWS, INC. All Rights Reserved.

Draw Your Attention

Pillar 5: Attentiveness

"The game of life is won or lost in the attention to detail."

- Robb Thompson

Late one night, awhile back, I sat in the office of a very successful businessman. The people who worked for this man, including his administrator, his business manager, and his accountant, surrounded his desk. All these people were trying to get their boss's attention so they could find out what he wanted them to do.

But I noticed that some type of miscommunication was occurring between that employer and the employees in his office. After several minutes of increasing frustration, the businessman suddenly turned to me and asked, *"Why can't I get what I want?"*

I felt sorry for the people in the room who heard that comment. But later, as I pondered the matter, I came to understand what this man meant. I realized that the character trait of *attentiveness* determines the outcome in many situations of life.

Just what is attentiveness? The word "attentive" or "attention" actually comes from the French word *attendere*, meaning *to wait, to stay, to hold, and to expect.* The Latin word *attentio* carries a slightly different meaning. It gives us the picture of a horse *perking up or twitching its ears,* as it gives its attention to something. Thus, we could say that attentiveness means *showing the worth of a person, an object, or an idea by giving it one's undivided concentration.*

Why is this attribute so significant? Because the outcome of our lives is not usually determined by the big things that we think are so important. On the contrary, it's the *details* (the small particulars of life to which

most people pay no attention) that will cause us either to win or to lose, in our pursuit of significant, productive lives. This truth cannot be overlooked: **The game of life is won or lost in the attention to detail.**

I remember the time I was invited for dinner at a couple's home. As we sat eating dinner, the wife got up from the dining room table to get her husband another serving of the main dish. As she left for the kitchen, she exclaimed to me, "Oh, he just loves this dish!"

But as soon as his wife was out of earshot, the husband said to me, "I've always hated this stuff. But she keeps making it and then expects me to eat it."

"Have you ever told her that you don't like it?" I asked.

"Well, yes, I've told her, but it's as if she doesn't hear. I don't ever want to eat this food again, but I can't say anything about it. If I do, she's going to think I hate everything else she does!"

Details Matter

This type of situation happens in every arena of life, not just in the home. It happens on the job. It happens between friends. It happens in civic affairs. People are not attentive to detail and, thus, fail to be what someone else actually wants or needs them to be.

Relationships are not the only arena affected by the character trait of attentiveness. Many goals, dreams, projects, and plans fail, due to the inattentiveness of those involved. Attention to detail can become quite tedious, wearisome, and unexciting — quickly boring to those who lack perseverance. But dreams seldom manifest without the steadfast, purposeful "plowing" through the reams of daily minutiae.

Often, we see people being very enthusiastic and attentive *at the start* of a big project. The excitement level is high, as the "big vision" of the undertaking is heralded. People jostle each other to squeeze in front of the cameras and be seen in the "ground breaking" ceremonies of life.

But where are these same people when all the publicity and fanfare have faded away? Where are they when it's actually time to roll up the sleeves and commence with the very unglamorous details of building something from scratch? When the days, weeks, and months roll by, it will only be those with dedication, determination, and dogged tenacity that will still be diligently attending to the necessary details.

Attentiveness ensures that an assignment is completed, long before you ever hear the words, "Mission accomplished." We cannot claim to be attentive if we do just *part* of our assignment. What if we underwent internal surgery, and the doctor put only *some* of our body parts back in place? Or what if we rebuilt the engine on our car and, afterward, found we had a couple of parts to spare? One thing is certain: "Mission *almost* accomplished" is not acceptable to a person of deep and continuously pursued character!

Attentiveness that is only half-heartedly given is negligence and disrespect. These issues become particularly serious when we are dealing with those whom we are to respect.

Attentiveness

If I were to choose one primary trait to possess, in order to multiply favor in my life, it would be the quality of *attentiveness to those in authority.* Whether it is one's father, mother, employer, president, or pastor, giving *meticulous attention* to the issues that matter to him or her will

bring an immediate flow of favor into one's life. It is an undeniable fact that **promotion is summoned to a person's life the moment he gives attention to detail.**

We will never receive a promotion through the avenue of a contrary, stubborn, or rebellious life. We will never be chosen for our passive resistance. We will never obtain the prize by countering our authority's instruction with a defiant, "But this is what *I* want to do."

We must determine to follow this principle of *attentiveness to leaders* throughout our lives, no matter what kind of circumstances we find ourselves in. As a result, our diligent attention to detail will bring us promotion, no matter how bleak it seems.

Give Others What They Want

There is another aspect to attentiveness that we must understand. When desiring to give someone a gift, we should not resort to choosing something *we* want them to have. We must give them something they actually want, because that is the gift that will be before them for some time (along with the remembrance of who gave it to them).

How can the giver know what a person actually wants? *By being attentive.* This is what will distinguish one individual from another. When an individual is more attentive to those he is responsible to, he will receive greater favor from them.

Now, mind you, a leader's favor toward one person, in particular, will likely make others *very* upset. (Of course, it shouldn't matter if everyone in the world is upset, as long as favor is coming to us directly from the boss!) We must not concern ourselves with the petty resentment of our peers — our assignment and attentiveness is not toward them. Our job

is to stay confident in the knowledge that, as we give ourselves to the details to which we've been assigned, success will be ours.

The Winning Key

Many people are scrambling to find an answer to this burning question: "How does a person become prosperous?" In the world today, people assume that prosperity is linked to money. But there are many people who have a great deal of money, yet are actually not prosperous.

When we choose to be attentive and faithful in whatever situation we find ourselves, we quickly discover *that* is the essence of prosperity. When a person is living in this kind of prosperity, it doesn't matter what anyone thinks or whether he has a dime in the bank — *he's going to win.*

What is the difference between a winner and a loser? Nothing but attention to detail. No matter how many people or situations try to destroy a person, attention to detail will continually cause him to rise back to the top. Why? Because a person who possesses the quality of attentiveness cannot be denied.

We live in a society where people continually neglect their responsibilities and then cry, "I'm a victim!" But a person can hide or cover up his neglected responsibilities for only so long. Without the quality of attentiveness, he may fill a slot, but he will never be called upon for promotion. To become truly valuable to others, a person *must* give attention to detail.

In every situation we face in life, we will continue to develop our character if we focus on the details. What are the little particulars that other people don't see or pay attention to? Whatever those details are, we must be attentive in taking care of them. Remember, **we won't be rewarded for**

our similarities to others; rather, we will be rewarded for our differences.

Constant attention to detail is certainly not easy or convenient. We will be tested continually. Are we going to hold on or are we going to let go? We must never let go of our larger vision, but at the same time, we must stay faithful and attentive to the details that will help bring that vision to pass.

How does a person best demonstrate the value, respect, and esteem that he holds toward someone? It is through his attentiveness. **The foundation of love is honor, and the demonstration of honor is attentiveness.** There is no love without honor, and there is no honor without attentiveness. Wherever an individual places the treasure of his time, energy, concentration, and affection, that is where his heart and future will abide.

To gain more than just a cursory knowledge of anything or anyone requires an in-depth, comprehensive thoroughness. Anyone can skim the surface and gain some knowledge about a subject. However, our value, regarding that knowledge, is measured only by the degree of our attentiveness to learn more. Wisdom and understanding are not attained by skimming. **True knowledge is gained only by offering someone our full attention.**

Concentration

The word "attention" implies a *consistent choice to deeply concentrate.* Concentration requires every part of a person. In order to be attentive to a particular someone, we must choose to gain the full picture of what that person is communicating to us. We must know what he wants and desires. We must give him our undivided attention and gain the inner picture that only vigilant observation can give us.

A person with undeveloped attentiveness only scans over the subject being discussed. His listening is distracted, his responses disconnected, and his understanding shallow. He doesn't really hear what the other person *wants* him to hear.

I remember a man who once told me, "I never raise my voice when I talk to people. I whisper."

"Why do you do that?" I asked.

"Because when you whisper, people have to give you their undivided attention, in order to hear what you are saying!"

When I heard that, I thought, "This man may have come up with a good idea for teaching people the indispensable quality of attentiveness!"

I realized, however, that this method is favorable only when the speaker has the benefit of the listeners in mind. If used in the hands of a prideful, self-centered person, this tactic becomes just another way to gather people around himself, giving him a false sense of self-importance.

Favor and promotion begin to chase us down when we look for the areas where others lack, and then choose to make up the slack. Our value is not in what we do *the same* as everyone else; it is in what we do *differently* than others.

It is hard to imagine how much it warms a person's heart to realize that someone has observed him carefully enough to know the things he likes and dislikes. It means so much to him when he sees someone make up the difference in the areas where he is lacking.

An employee pleases his superior beyond words when he listens intently to the directive given and then carries it out to the last detail, without complaint or procrastination. This is the person who receives promotions and favor in the workplace. The employer relaxes when he hands

out an assignment to this employee, knowing that there is no need to wonder whether or not he is going to do the job correctly.

An employee who fits this description is a rare find for a person in leadership. Too many people complete ninety percent of a given assignment and then just quit, never finishing what they started.

But it isn't how we start any race in life that matters; it's how we finish. Every one of us can be a great starter, but very few of us really know how to finish. And where does the breakdown usually lie, when people fail to finish what they have been assigned? *It's in their lack of attention to detail.*

It's easy to see why attentiveness is the key that determines how far a person will be promoted!

Consideration

Consideration is simply applying the traits of attentiveness and sensitivity to our interpersonal relationships, especially when it comes to transparent and truthful communication. We have to *consider* our relationships. One of the greatest mistakes an individual could ever make is to assume that people can handle what he has on his heart to tell them. Before he ever speaks, he must consider who they are, what they are facing, and where they are in their journey of character. **In order to bring transformation to this world, every relationship requires the deepest of commitments and consideration.**

Let's talk about how we can develop attentiveness in our various relationships, whether at home, on the job, or with the leaders in life.

First, when someone addresses us, we must not allow ourselves to be preoccupied. We should put down what we're doing, face the person, look in his eyes, and give him our full attention.

Secondly, we can't allow our relationships to remain meaningless and superficial. We must care enough to find out what the other person is facing, and then help him to solve his problem. As we listen to him, it's important to stay attentive to hear even some of his unspoken needs, for our rewards in life are in direct proportion to the problems that we are able to solve for others.

Thirdly, if a person in authority is giving us an instruction, we don't want to be casual about it. Our attentive attitudes should always convey to our superiors that we are poised to get up and do exactly what they have asked us to do, as soon as they have finished speaking.

This kind of attentiveness is such a rare quality in today's society. People are so preoccupied and self-absorbed. They're not listening. They don't ask questions or clarify instruction. And then, when they make a mistake or do something wrong, rarely do they ever say, "I'm sorry — we'll do this over again at no charge." Instead, they say, "Oops! Well, you have a great attitude, so this will be all right, won't it?" In other words, they expect those with good attitudes to accept and pay for their inferior work!

But that is not the way to live. We must make the quality decision to be continual learners who are attentive to detail and always interested in what others are saying. Our time should be managed in such a way that those with whom we have relationship realize how important they are to us.

Attentiveness is a daily habit that causes us to focus on that which truly matters to others. Since we can only be attentive to one thing at a

time, it is vital that we stop focusing on things that don't matter and choose, instead, to focus on the most important things of life, especially the relationships we've been given.

Here is an important truth about life: *Relationships are the only things that will last.* Cars rust; money fades away; and popularity wanes. *Nothing* matters except relationships. So, we cannot allow ourselves to be quick to break them; in fact, we must do everything in our power to keep them!

An attentive person fights *for* his relationships, not *against* them. He gives them his attention. He takes notes. When he hears the way someone thinks, he writes it down. If something is important enough for a person to bring up in a conversation, the attentive listener knows it is important enough to write down. He is quick to hear and slow to speak.

This character quality of attentiveness is to be applied to every area of life. It doesn't work to demonstrate outstanding attentiveness on the job, yet neglect our marriages or our roles as parents. As we consistently choose to concentrate on what is most important, not only to us but also to others — paying close attention to the details that make all the difference — we will put ourselves on the road to promotion in every endeavor we undertake!

Seven Ways to Be More Attentive

1. Don't just hear — listen.

Discover what is considered a job well done. Listen, so you can give your superior what he really wants.

2. Write it down.

When you write down your instructions, you show that you value what is being said, and that you will do what you are told. Don't trust your memory. It is estimated that the short-term memory will only store something for forty seconds. Always have a paper and a pen ready. Your boss will be more detailed when he sees you writing; and the more detailed his instructions, the more excellence you can apply to fulfilling his request.

3. Interpret it back to him.

Always repeat back what you thought you heard the speaker say. You may have heard something other than what was meant. When you reiterate what was said, your boss will know you understand, or he'll correct your misunderstandings. This step will save you time in the long run.

4. Ask him to prioritize his instructions.

When given a list of things to do, ask which items are most important. Complete them in order of importance. What you think is important may not be as important to your employer.

5. Act quickly.

Get to work immediately, remembering that accuracy is more important than speed. Combine both as much as possible.

6. Report back.

Keep your boss up to date on your progress. Lack of communication breeds uncertainty. You should never have to be asked for a progress report. Make it your responsibility to communicate to your supervisor.

7. Never complain.

You may say, "I never say anything negative to my boss or my fellow employees." I commend you on that, but complaining doesn't always have to be voiced. It can be communicated by body language. How do you respond when your boss gives you an instruction? Do you smile and welcome it, or do you show that you are not happy to hear what he has to say? Your body language makes a big difference.

Life Lesson

One day, a woodcutter took his grandson into the forest for his first experience in selecting and cutting oak trees. These they would later sell to the boat builders. As they walked along, the woodcutter explained that the purpose of each tree is contained in its natural shape: some are straight for planks, some have the proper curves for the ribs of a boat, and some are tall for masts. The woodcutter told his grandson that by paying attention to the details of each tree, and with experience in recognizing these characteristics, someday he, too, might become the woodcutter of the forest.

A little way into the forest, the grandson saw an old oak tree that had never been cut. The boy asked his grandfather if he could cut it down because it was useless for boat building — there were no straight limbs, the trunk was short and gnarled, and the curves were going the wrong way. "We could cut it down for firewood," the grandson said. "At least then, it will be of some use to us." The woodcutter replied that, for now, they should be about their work, cutting the proper trees for the boat builders; maybe later they could return to the old oak tree.

After a few hours of cutting the huge trees, the grandson grew tired and asked if they could stop for a rest in some cool shade. The woodcutter took his grandson over to the old oak tree, where they rested against its trunk, in the cool shade beneath its twisted limbs. After they had rested a while, the woodcutter explained to his grandson the necessity of attentive awareness and recognition of everything in the forest and in the world. Some things are readily apparent, like the tall, straight trees; other things are less apparent, requiring closer attention, like recognition of the proper curves in the limbs. And some things might initially appear to have no purpose at all, like the gnarled old oak tree.

The woodcutter stated, "You must learn to pay careful attention, every day, so you can recognize and discover the purpose God has for everything in creation. For it is this old oak tree, which you so quickly deemed useless except for firewood, that now allows us to rest against its trunk amidst the coolness of its shade.

"Remember, grandson, not everything is as it first appears. Be patient, pay attention, recognize, and discover."[1]

"I CAN'T GIVE YOU MY FULL ATTENTION, BOB, BUT I CAN GIVE YOU MY ALMOST CONSTANT PARTIAL ATTENTION."

Don't Put Foot In Mouth

Pillar 6: Discretion

"Let your own discretion be your tutor; suit the action to the word, the word to the action."

- William Shakespeare

Let's say a person has worked hard to develop the character attributes we have already discussed. He is ready to say, "Integrity, truthfulness, self-control, compliance, compassion, attentiveness, and respect for those in higher places in life are qualities that I possess." What can this person do to make sure all these attributes are firmly fixed in his life? Is there a trait that puts the finishing touches on his character?

Yes — that trait is called *discretion.*

Discretion is like the finishing school for one's character. It is also the invisible glue that holds together all the other elements of noble character and keeps them permanently set inside one's heart.

An individual might be a person of great truthfulness; however, if he doesn't understand discretion, he will become so brash that no one will be able to tolerate him. Someone might be a person of great integrity; but unless he is also a person of discretion, he will come across as greatly arrogant. Attentiveness is an essential character trait; nevertheless, if used without discretion, it causes one to become an intrusive nuisance. In this way, discretion becomes the governor of all the other character traits that are developed in our lives.

Discretion has so many facets that it cannot be easily defined with a simple explanation or description. Let's look at a number of different definitions, as we try to encompass the full meaning of this word.

The dictionary defines "discretion" as *being careful about what one says or does; the ability to keep silent.* The dictionary also says that this quality is *regulated by one's own choice.* For instance, when the law says that something is "left up to one's discretion," that means it is left up to a person's choice. We cannot decide what another person's discretion is, for it has to do with his own conclusion to the question, "How do I think this situation should be approached?"

Someone is a person of discretion because he chooses to be so. However, discretion isn't a character trait that we either do or do not possess. Rather, it is a quality that lives *in degrees* inside every person.

Other words that help fill out the meaning of the word "discretion" are *calculating, careful, considerate, guarded, and safe,* as well as *the concept of exercising precaution, foresight, forethought, restraint, and common sense.*

People of discretion are calculated, careful, and considerate. They are safe to be around because *they strategically choose restraint.* They are people of precaution who will test the integrity of a situation before ever going into it.

A person of discretion possesses:

- **The wisdom to avoid damaging attitudes, words, and actions**
- **The ability to give insightful counsel to others**
- **An intuitive perception of the nature and meaning of things; this perception results in sound judgment and wise decision-making**
- **The ability to discern universal truth and to apply it to human disposition and conduct**

The Picture of Discretion

Can discretion be learned? Yes, it *can;* and the best way to do so is by keeping quiet! Even a fool is thought to be wise and discerning when he stays quiet.

At one time or another, we have all wondered why certain people act the way they do. This is especially true when we encounter individuals who always seem to say abrasive, offensive things, with no concern for how they may be hurting or discouraging others. What is the source of such poor behavior? It is a lack of discretion.

Discretion is the guard that protects an individual from the calamity of a multitude of words. A person of discretion understands how to accurately discern a situation so that he says no more than he is asked to say. At times, he even conveys his heart with nothing more than a look. He is parsimonious, for he uses his words very sparingly. As a result, when he finally does choose to speak, his words tend to carry greater weight, among those who hear, than do the words of those who voice their opinions without reservation.

A person of discretion can talk to everyone in the room without telling all he knows, because he understands that only a fool speaks his whole mind. That doesn't mean a person of discretion is secretive. He is actually a warm, open, loving person who genuinely cares for people. He just has the wisdom to know what to say and what *not* to say. He exercises restraint, not because he's muzzled by fear of any sort, but because he realizes that there is a time and a season for all things. **In every situation, the discreet individual knows the attitudes, words, and actions that are right, honorable, and just to act upon.**

A person of discretion understands the boundaries he must respect in the life of another. When it comes to speaking the truth and giving correction, he knows how far he can go, in a person's life, before he risks causing offense or breaking the individual's spirit.

People may, at times, tell their friends, "Oh, you can tell me the truth. Go ahead — say to me whatever is on your heart."

But discerning friends must often reply, "No, I can't tell you the truth, because, earnestly, you don't want to know the truth. You want me to tell you what you *want* to hear. You're looking for someone to agree with you and tell you that you're okay."

This scenario has plagued my life. I have come to realize that people generally surround themselves with those who are cheerleaders rather than those who represent a voice of reason. This has resulted in situations that none of us want to endure, but we are now being made to face. Our government, businesses, marriages, children, friends, and associates have all tried to figure out what we wanted to hear, and then gave it to us, resulting in a world that is not only in need of repair but just may be taken from us, unless we are willing to adopt some very harsh measures. May Heaven intervene on our behalf.

In spite of the fact that most people would benefit greatly by hearing the truth, people of discretion refrain from just blurting it out without concern for the possible fallout of offense or hurt emotions. They are seeking to walk out the greatest of all lives, the life of discretion; and that means they must know how to avoid overstepping the boundaries of another person's life. The primary concern of a discreet individual is that his attitudes and words fit the need of the moment and are perceived as honorable and gracious.

Exercising Foresight

The person of discretion understands that future consequences are the result of present actions. He is a person of forethought, thinking about his decisions in ten-year time frames. He ponders, *"How is this decision going to cost me or benefit me in the long run?"* Based on the answer to that question, he then decides if the long-term benefits are worth the short-term pain.

Exercising foresight, he seriously considers and then avoids certain situations, because of their long-term consequences. He understands that some actions will cause more long-term pain than short-term gain.

Individuals who lack discretion don't think with foresight. They just want to be comfortable in the present, and they don't really care about the consequences that they, or others, might suffer in the future. They think, "If doing this will just relieve the pressure I am under right now, who cares about what it might mean five years from now?"

If the road to excellence gets tough, the person of discretion understands that he can't just abort his ethics to make things easier on himself. He is committed to *long-term rewards* and is, therefore, willing to endure *short-term pain.*

Some people readily abandon their inner ideals for selfish motives. They have an attitude that continually says, "It's all about me." They think, "It doesn't matter what I do, so I'll just get rid of this relationship. How I treat this situation isn't the issue. After all, I have to take care of myself!"

When a person starts thinking like that, it's only a matter of time before he reaps a negative harvest. But that harvest won't return at a time when it's convenient for him. It will come at a time when he doesn't

want it to show up in his life, because the Law of Sowing and Reaping doesn't give a person a choice in the timing of his consequences.

Discreet men and women use judicious consideration when it comes to their interaction with others. They often decide, "I'm not going to say that, because if I do, this person might take it wrong and get offended." Or they conclude, "If I say this, I'll give people the wrong idea about what I really mean; so I'm not going to say it."

When they have to make a decision that pertains to someone else, they will first put themselves in the other's position. Only then, from that understanding, will they make their decision, ever aware of what it will mean to the other person. This kind of forethought is very rare and, therefore, a quality that is highly sought-after. When we meet people like that, they will always bring a smile to our face.

If we choose to become discrete, forethought has to be a part of our daily existence. We realize that if we ever discard principle, many of those who look up to our example would also discard it. A discreet individual does not think about his own short-term comforts. He continually chooses to do the right thing for the long-term good of the people he is called to serve, doing all that he can to preserve them from dangerous situations.

Discretion Detours Destruction

In our pursuit of impeccable character, we need to know how to detour around dangerous people and situations. King David instructed his son, Solomon:

> My son, pay attention to my wisdom; lend your ear to my understanding, that you may preserve discretion, and your lips may keep knowledge.

> For the lips of an immoral woman drip honey, and her mouth is smoother than oil; but in the end she is bitter as wormwood, sharp as a two-edged sword.[1]

The Hebrew word for *discretion*, in this quote, is the word *mezimmah.* It refers to *the ability to devise innovative, witty, insightful plans.* So how does this word fit, in this context?

David told his son that, in the end, the immoral woman's words are as bitter as wormwood (a deadly poison) and as dangerous as a snakebite. In other words, David was saying, "Solomon, when an immoral woman attempts to draw you away from your inner values of honor and virtue, be insightful enough to remember that the ultimate harvest she offers you is death."

This Hebrew word for discretion, then, has to do with one's ability to detour around such people — individuals who would like to find access to a person's life and destroy him.

Discretion avoids situations that could compromise its commitment to strong moral fortitude. A person of discretion looks at a potentially dangerous situation and sees where that path leads. Then he thinks, "I know that within eighteen months, that would destroy my family, so I'm not going that direction!" However, a man who lacks discretion doesn't consider the long-term consequences of compromise.

A discreet individual distinguishes right from wrong *and then chooses what is right,* no matter what the cost. It's likely that we all know people who have the ability to discern the difference between right and wrong, yet don't choose *to do* what is right because of the influence of others. When examining this most difficult of all scenarios, we find that most individuals compromise because doing what is right, at this level, is not expedient for them and neither advances nor prolongs their agendas.

We must never allow this type of character flaw to invade our environment. The moment we attribute our choices to anyone else's actions is the moment we have allowed our lives to get out of our control. We must *never* allow anything but principle to control our lives, for our futures are determined by the decisions we make.

Regard Discretion

Let's look again at the instruction young Solomon was given by his father:

> My son, pay attention to my wisdom; lend your ear to my understanding, that you may *preserve discretion*, and your lips may keep knowledge.

Another word for the term "preserve" is *regard*. Most don't really *regard discretion.* They may want to be discreet about their own private matters, but they *don't* want to be discreet about the private matters of others.

A person who regards discretion would rather consider another person's needs than to consider his own. He understands that *it is greater to choose to serve than it is to be approached to serve.* He fulfills the wishes of others before those wishes are ever expressed. Because he continually remains in the servant's role, he has people chasing him, trying to figure out what his next step will be. That is a *much* better position to be in than to hear people continually say, "You failed to do this!" or "You didn't do that right."

Seeing What Others Don't See

A person of discretion focuses on what others ignore. He concentrates on what is happening *inside* people, rather than on what he sees on the outside.

Many people will say that things are going great in their lives. Then they seem to drop out of sight, and they aren't seen for three or four months. And when we finally do see them again, we find out their lives are a wreck!

But still, they will protest, "Oh, no, we're really doing fine."

"You're really doing fine? What about those bankruptcy papers you have in your hand?"

Such individuals need a reality check, regarding their personal integrity. Meanwhile, a person of discretion is able to look beyond the external and discern what is *really* working on the inside of another person — beyond what the natural eye can see. And because he focuses on the internal, he is better able to help move the external circumstances to a higher plane.

Guiding Our Affairs

A good man deals with others graciously. He conducts his relationships with understanding, and he guides his affairs with discretion.

Another meaning of the word "discretion" is *giving a judgment or making a verdict.* The person of discretion guides his affairs with good judgment. He makes wise verdicts, and he doesn't backtrack on them later. He cannot be persuaded to change his mind once he knows what to do.

Let me give an example of what it means to guide one's affairs with discretion. A discreet individual might enter into an agreement with one person that he wouldn't even consider entering with another. Why? Because he will not obligate an individual to keep his word if he has no capacity to do so.

For instance, he may tell certain people to whom he has lent money, "Listen, I want you to forget about the money you borrowed from me. It's fine. Consider the matter closed."

On the other hand, there may be other people whose debt he will not forgive. It might even look like he *should* release them from their debt obligation, but he won't do it. Why not? Because he suspects that is exactly what they *planned* for him to do when they borrowed the money in the first place! They were just waiting for the lender to let them off the hook — so he doesn't do it. If he did, he would just be giving in to their lack of faithfulness. People like that have to be held accountable to keep their word. All this lender has done is guide his affairs with discretion.

When we keep lending money to people who don't pay us back, we demonstrate a lack of discretion. The man of character doesn't lend to people who do not pay their debts. Otherwise, he wouldn't be lending; he'd be *giving*. He understands that one doesn't lend to someone who doesn't have the opportunity or the wherewithal to pay him back.

Most of us have probably lent to people unwisely. We have even given to people who have acted foolishly all their lives — those who survive by leeching off anyone who lacks the discretion to say *no*. These people will eventually come to the place where they have no more money and no one left to borrow from. At that point, their world will cave in, and it won't be pretty. We would be wiser to allow them to take the hit *sooner* rather

than later, so that life's hard lessons wouldn't hurt them (or our pocketbook) as severely!

When a person guides his affairs with discretion, bad news doesn't get to him. Even in the worst of times, he knows that wisdom will guide him, and discretion will lead him to success. In the end, his life will be full of honor because he walked in discretion through every situation.

Protect the Treasure

It is possible to be a very bright person and, yet, not be very wise. However, a person of discretion is always a wise individual. He may not have a lot of brains, but he does know how to guide his affairs with wisdom.

Because **discretion celebrates the unequaled value of wisdom,** it will produce treasures in a person's life. However, if a person values finances more than he values wisdom, that person won't be able to sleep well at night. Only discretion will give an individual peace, as he rests in the knowledge that he has done the right thing with his treasures.

That's why we don't have to spend our energies protecting what others consider to be treasures. We need only to guard and protect this quality of discretion in our lives.

We have to fight to keep our commitment to principle in this life because, when promotion comes, it often comes with this question: *"Do you want the promotion, or do you want be principled?"* Most people will go for the promotion, if they have to choose. But we must say, "No, I don't want that kind of promotion; I'll take the promotion that a principled lifestyle brings."

"Yes, but you could have the money now. You could buy a boat and

spend all your free time out on the water having a good time!"

It doesn't matter. Principle must mean more to us than a boat or anything else money can buy.

What about the person who chooses his promotion over his commitment to integrity? When he dies, the question won't be, "How did his life influence others?" The only question people will ask is, "Who inherited the boat?" This person gave up his personal ethics and integrity to get that boat and, in the end, someone else will get it for nothing! Now, *that* is foolish behavior!

Knowledge + Discretion = Wisdom

When one immerses himself in principles of wisdom, knowledge, and understanding almost every day, he is, more than likely, amazed by people who persist in doing foolish things that can only hurt them in the long run.

People who do foolish things often rationalize, "Well, this will take the pressure off me *today*; and that's what I need!"

Usually, when we make a decision that is designed to relieve present pressure, we live to regret that decision, for it often leads to unnecessary pain. Instead of freeing ourselves from pressure, we only multiply and extend it; then, we must deal with the fruit of our own foolishness!

That is why it's so helpful to listen to wise principles every day. Everything good in our lives can be traced back to the regular intake of wise principles and precepts.

We don't have to be real smart. It's not necessary to have an edge over anyone else. We just need to find a wise principle and do it. It's

really no big deal. Anyone can do it, because **discretion turns knowledge into wise counsel.** If a person would just listen to and follow principled instruction on a regular basis, with a determination to *do* whatever he hears, his life would become very different in a short amount of time.

THE VALUE OF RESTRAINT

Discretion includes the ability to control destructive emotions. The truth is, our emotions have gotten us into more trouble than our actions could ever get us out of!

For instance, a boy tells a girl that he loves her, and her emotions get all involved. Nine months later, she has a "love child"! Then she finds out that the love he proclaimed isn't love anymore. However, she still has a love child that will be with her for life.

We must avoid making our choices based upon a person at his best. Instead, we should observe him at his worst. We must watch and see how he treats other people when he is under pressure, realizing that he will treat us no differently. A person of forethought considers, "What's the *worst* that a person with this kind of character could ever do to me?" That is much wiser than thinking, "What's the *best* he could do for me if he's having a good day and comes through with some of his promises?"

Here is another fact about controlling emotions: A person may have wisdom in giving counsel to others, yet lack the ability to control his own emotions. His emotions lead him instead of the other way around.

It is often wise for us to hold back our anger and overlook another's mistake. On the other hand, it is important to know when to speak and to confront an issue. Too often, we overlook things we shouldn't overlook,

but then spark huge battles over issues we should just ignore!

It is the character trait of *discretion* that will reliably guide us in these matters and give us the ability to control destructive emotions in all situations.

To Speak or Not to Speak

A person of discretion intuitively knows when to speak and when to be silent — when to get involved in a situation and when to stay out — because he understands the jurisdictions of the people who are in his life. If they are within *his* jurisdiction of responsibility, he considers the possibility of confronting the issue. If they are not within his jurisdiction, he understands that he does not know everything he needs to know in order to make a wise decision. Therefore, he won't allow himself to have an opinion.

Many people do not follow this principle. They neglect the areas for which *they* are personally responsible and, at the same time, spend all their energies forming opinions about matters for which *someone else* is responsible.

The person of discretion refuses to do that. He stays out of other people's business. He only has an opinion about the things for which *he* has been made responsible. He understands that if he wastes his time developing an opinion about someone else's jurisdiction, he wouldn't be taking care of what belongs to him.

I have heard it best said that to meddle in an affair that is not our responsibility is like grabbing a dog by the ears! If we grab a dog by the

ears, he is going to bite us. And if we intrusively meddle in someone else's business, we are going to get bit in that situation as well.

Our society is sorely lacking people who will exercise discretion, in deciding what to do in any given situation. We need to be people who are intelligent about our choices, remembering that it is often best to overlook another's mistakes. We must learn when to say something and when to keep quiet, discerning which battles to pick and which ones to pass up. As we develop this aspect of discretion in our lives and refuse to fight battles for which we are not responsible, we will avoid unnecessary grief and keep ourselves on the path to building ethical character.

If a person decides to pursue the finishing touch of discretion, he takes his place among a small remnant of principled people, for very few possess this valuable trait. There is plenty of room for another name on the official "people of discretion" plaque!

Discretion lives in constant preparation for the hour when an honorable purpose summons it to action. Every honorable purpose is searching for men and women of discretion and noble character to champion its cause. Have we invested the necessary time to prepare ourselves for the purpose of our lives? Are we ready for our defining moment upon the stage of life? When the call to action sounds, it will then be too late to prepare. We must do what is necessary *today* to ensure that we are prepared and ready for the hour when our honorable purpose summons us to action!

Life Lesson

A man walked up to the secretary to ask for an apartment application. She tersely replied, "The deadline was yesterday. I can't give you one." The man, perceiving her stubbornness, politely left the office. He proceeded to write her an email, but didn't identify himself as the man in the office until the end of the letter.

He first acknowledged the goal of the company — to make a profit from its tenants. He commented that he understood the necessity to have reliable tenants who abide by policies and pay their rent on time. He then said that he wished to be that kind of tenant, and that the company would benefit greatly from his consistency and respect for the property. He identified himself as the man from the office and requested her graciousness in allowing him to apply, reminding her that it was in the company's best interest.

Upon reading the email, she was so impressed by the man's eloquence and humility that she promptly sent a reply, inviting him to pick up an application.[2]

SHOOTING YOURSELF IN THE FOOT WHILE YOUR FOOT IS IN YOUR MOUTH IS DIFFICULT, BUT BY GOLLY, YOU MANAGED TO DO IT IN THERE.
CONFERENCE ROOM
10-7
© 2010 GarLanCo/Distributed by Universal Uclick
WISE/ ALDRICH

Bringing It Home

Pillar 7: Understanding

"I've come to believe that all my past failure and frustration were actually laying the foundation for the understandings that have created the new level of living I now enjoy."

- Anthony Robbins

Pursuing ethical character becomes an exercise in futility unless one knows how to *apply* its wisdom to the business of daily living, in a practical, pragmatic way. *An understanding heart* is a key factor in having the ability to readily translate instruction into personal discipline, good conduct, and behavior that is right, just, and fair.

The proof of ethical character is the development and demonstration of an understanding heart. When people begin to develop understanding, harshness and arrogance leave their lives. They aren't so judgmental anymore. They become more interested in *demonstrating* their goodness through their actions, than they are in *talking* about their goodness. All of this comes as a result of acquiring and achieving *understanding,* through a steady diet of principled instruction.

Those who have spent time studying the ways of the wise already know much more than they realize. They are a lot smarter than they think! But embracing the trait of understanding opens their eyes to the fact that simply *knowing* something is not what makes a difference in life. Things begin to change only when one starts *acting on what he knows.*

As we pursue truth and wisdom, diligently guarding them within our hearts, the words of our own mouths will begin to bring us understanding. We will begin to speak with a depth of discernment that we may not even realize we possess (although our life experiences may not yet reflect the level of wisdom and understanding that we have gained from our studies).

Wisdom in Action

A person of understanding knows that he must link his wisdom to his conduct. We cannot speak principles of wisdom to others and simultaneously neglect to act upon wisdom ourselves.

By the same token, we should never listen to a person who doesn't *do* what he says. Someone like that has nothing to lose in giving us advice. If his wisdom and understanding aren't good enough for him, they aren't good enough for others, either!

Our lives will greatly benefit if we listen only to people who are willing to risk everything for what is right and true. People like that will put everything they are on the line, in order to get the right thing to happen in *another's* life. Those are the people we need to pursue, when desiring to gain understanding.

If a person is in error, in any area of his life, *understanding* will correct him, teach him how to stop doing what is wrong, and show him how to begin doing what is right. If he is an employee, understanding will show him how to best please those to whom he is responsible. If he is a parent, understanding will give him direction in raising good children. If the individual is a husband or a wife, understanding will add peace and life to his or her marriage.

Too many couples spend their married lives arguing. Finally, after being married for thirty years, they get to the point where they decide just to put up with each other for the rest of their lives, because they don't want to start over again in another relationship.

There are so few individuals in this world who even *want* to understand their spouses. That's why it's so important for husbands and wives

to seek to be gifts to each other, by pursuing understanding in the marriage relationship.

For husbands who value character, there is no alternative but to become men of principle and lead their families. If a husband is not a man of understanding, integrity, and principle within his home, that home will fail. Likewise, the home will fail if the wife does not choose to be understanding. And when the parents fail to take their roles in the home, their children are the ones who will pay the price.

A person of character strives daily to gain more understanding. He will actually search more for *understanding*, in a situation, than for answers. Discovering an answer simply means that closure is now available to any given situation, whereas understanding is something he can take into *all* areas of life.

THROUGH THE EYES OF UNDERSTANDING

Understanding comes as we begin to pursue principle. As we engage ourselves in sound knowledge, wisdom will often reveal, in little glimpses, the things we need to know. When we see one of those small glimpses, we need to revisit it again and again, until we finally get complete understanding.

We need understanding so we can accurately interpret and apply principled guidelines. We also need understanding so we can see the situations we face from a deeper perspective, not just from a subjective point of view. If we look at life through our own limited perspective, we will never understand it, for genuine insight lies only in what *truth* has to say about any given subject.

A person of understanding is a person of wisdom, insight, wise counsel, and discretion; therefore, he does not judge only by what he sees. **Reserving judgment for the appropriate time clothes a man with understanding.**

A person of understanding doesn't look at situations as they *seem* to be; after all, people can make things look the way they want them to look. Instead of looking at the outward appearance to discern the truth of a situation, one who exercises understanding examines the heart of the situation.

In order to guide our affairs with understanding, we need to know why things are said and why people do the things they do. But we can't understand these things by using our own reasoning abilities. That is why we must never judge by what we see or what we hear. Rather, we must perceive with *pure* judgment. This judgment is only possible when we *understand* the principles operating in the situation.

Welcome Instruction

Individuals who possess understanding realize that they must be corrected, at times, because it is vital that they become accurate in every area of life. However, most people don't want to be corrected. They resent correction and simply don't want to change. They don't realize that if they live without correction, their lives will produce nothing.

Understanding willingly accepts responsibility for its behavior. After receiving just one simple word of correction, a man of *understanding* will readily change and improve. He will grow in character through the correction. He understands that, in order to become the best person he can be, there will be times when he must be corrected. Conversely, one could

embarrass a show-off a hundred times, and he still won't change!

Though we all need periodic adjustment and guidance from wise leaders, that doesn't mean we can put the responsibility for the outcome of our lives on these most valuable of all people. We must always be willing to take responsibility for the outcome of our own lives. Only as we are willing to take responsibility *for* our lives will we be able to gain the necessary understanding *about* our lives.

Problem-Solver Extraordinaire

Understanding will greatly enhance our problem-solving abilities. We don't have to get along famously with others if we're willing to solve their problems. They will accept our little personality quirks, as long as we are willing to take care of that which has, up until now, remained unanswered.

Always keep in mind that **our value to others is in direct proportion to the problems we are willing to solve for them.** When each of us walks into a room, people will either think, *"Here comes a solution,"* or *"Oh, no — here comes another problem!"*

You see, we are either solving problems or creating problems, every day of our lives. We cannot be neutral. This makes life very simple. When our goal is to serve people, we don't need to try to figure out their individual personalities. All we need to remember is that the greatest among us must be the servant of all.

What should a person do when he wants to obtain favor from those who can help him grow in understanding? He must look within and search for his potential contribution. He must ask himself, *"How am I*

different from the myriad of others who desire the attention of great men and women? What can I bring that no one else can?" A person's unique gift will make room for him and bring him before great influencers.

The greater the individuals that we access, the greater will be the wisdom that is deposited into our lives. A gift (referring to any type of unique contribution) will get us in front of great men and women, but it will not *keep* us there. It is only the wisdom we are able to *embrace* that will keep us in the presence of greatness. Understanding will guide us in applying and exercising that wisdom.

We will only be remembered for the problems we have solved or the problems we have caused. If we would sit back and evaluate our past performance in the different areas of life, more than likely we would discover that we have been solving fewer problems than we thought we were. If so, we need to start making the needed adjustments right away. The moment we create more problems than we solve is the moment we have become unnecessary.

For instance, if an employee has a chronic bad attitude, it is only a matter of time before he is replaced. He is sitting upon a lit fuse, concerning the outcome of his position in the workplace.

Why is this true? It's very simple. It is unnatural for a business-person to maintain a painful relationship. As soon as he can find someone who will do the job without the pain, he will get rid of the painful relationship. So, it is up to that employee to become a problem-*solver* instead of a problem-*creator*— and the same principle holds true in every area of life.

THE REWARDS

What are the results and rewards of developing an understanding heart? *First, we learn to walk in compliance.* As we discussed earlier, compliance is an absolutely crucial attribute of any successful individual; it is an essential pillar built upon our character foundation. We could go so far as to say **it is impossible to be noncompliant and still become victorious over the challenges in life.**

It is a fact that the world celebrates the notion that "I did it my way." But if we insist on doing everything our way, we are building our plans on shifting sand, and they will eventually come to nothing.

It is a wise individual who refuses to argue with the truth of ethical principle. If principle says that lying is wrong at all times, then lying is wrong at all times. If principle says that a man's gift makes room for him, then that's the way it is. Someone might say, "That isn't fair to some people." But we cannot disregard ethical principles simply because they seem unfair or difficult to follow. Our only concern is that we get better at quickly complying with principle, every day of our lives.

We need to separate ourselves from people and situations that could draw us away from adhering to principle. In order to make sure our foundation is strong, we must dismantle our lives, cut out anything that is the least bit unethical, and then put our lives back together again, according to proven principles. If we fail to do so, we put ourselves in danger of extreme loss and failure.

That is what happened to the king whose name was Solomon. He became very successful and well-known, as the king of Israel, because he possessed unparalleled wisdom and understanding. However, by the end of his life, he had lost his understanding. Why? Because he could not

separate himself from his own opinion. Instead, he allowed it to draw him away from the wise principle he had once known. This became a tragic end for a king who had been so great.

Understand this: Whatever we do on the outside demonstrates what we have already done in our inner life. We can't say, "I have high moral values," and then go out and party with those who don't. Seventeenth century philosopher, John Locke, once said, *"I have always thought the actions of men the best interpreters of their thoughts."* If we are going to be principled people, we will be principled twenty-four hours a day, seven days a week.

Older people *should* possess more understanding than younger generations. However, in modern society, that isn't always the case. Many of our elders have not lived their lives in compliance to an ethical standard. If we will hold on to and obey honorable precepts and principles, we will walk in more understanding than everyone around us, regardless of our age.

When we live a life of understanding, we also reap the benefits of sensible living. One aspect of sensible living is that we remain silent when it comes to speaking negatively about others. When someone wants to know what we think of a certain person, we most often don't need to say anything if the answer is negative. The other person can hear more from what we *don't* say than he can ever hear from what we do. All he has to do is listen to the volumes of silence!

The second result of developing an understanding heart is *the ability to distinguish and follow the right path, in any given situation.* Understanding will lead us to say, "In every situation, I consider character and integrity to be the right choice. I follow the ethical way of doing

things and hate every other way that has nothing to do with what is true and honorable."

Understanding ensures that the voice of principle means more than the voice of excuse. It helps us to separate ourselves from people who make excuses for their failures. Understanding warns us to avoid those who make shady deals with one another, in an attempt to make things work. We set ourselves up for failure when we link ourselves to such individuals. But if we will determine to build our lives only on noble precepts, then we will still be standing, even when others fall.

The third reward of nurturing an understanding heart is *the enjoyment of a good life.* **A person of understanding is continually built up, refreshed, and renewed by the wellspring of his virtuous life.** Abundance and success are the signatures of every enterprise to which he sets his hand.

A Lack of Understanding

We've seen some of the benefits of developing an understanding heart. But what are the results of a *lack* of understanding? The primary result is *foolish behavior.* A person who lacks understanding commits stupid errors in judgment that can adversely affect the outcome of his entire life.

For instance, a man void of understanding has no qualms over committing adultery. He is easily seduced away from moral principle, not realizing the serious consequences of his actions. He's like an animal that races straight into a trap.

Why is a person who lacks understanding so easily pulled away from principle? Because he starts listening to others and believing what they say over what known and provable truth says. The only way to keep a per-

son from falling into that trap is by making sure that personal integrity and virtue mean more to him than the words of others. This individual *understands* that he is preserved from life-ruining traps by ***refusing to participate in any endeavor that promises future regret.***

The bottom line is this: An understanding heart is the key to experiencing one's best life and to reaching one's dreams and destiny. It is a treasure of unspeakable worth that only a few persistent seekers uncover. But to those who find it and, without apology or compromise, raise it high, as the crowning pediment of all the mighty pillars of character we've discussed, a life of unspeakable fulfillment awaits!

Life Lesson

One month before signing the Emancipation Proclamation, President Lincoln sent a long message to Congress, which was largely routine, but also proposed controversial measures such as voluntary colonization of slaves and compensated emancipation.

Lincoln devoted so much attention to preparing the message that his friend, David Davis, said, "Mr. Lincoln's whole soul is absorbed in his plan of remunerative emancipation." The concluding paragraphs, shown below, demonstrate Lincoln's passion for this plan and contain some of the most famous statements he ever wrote. Composer, Aaron Copeland, used excerpts in his evocative "Lincoln Portrait."

"I do not forget the gravity which should characterize a paper addressed to the Congress of the nation by the Chief Magistrate of the nation. Nor do I forget that some of you are my seniors, nor that many of you have more experience than I, in the conduct of public affairs. Yet I trust that, in view of the great responsibility resting upon me, you will

perceive no want of respect yourselves, in any undue earnestness I may seem to display.

"Is it doubted, then, that the plan I propose, if adopted, would shorten the war, and thus lessen its expenditure of money and of blood? Is it doubted that it would restore the national authority and national prosperity, and perpetuate both indefinitely? Is it doubted that we here — Congress and Executive — can secure its adoption? Will not the good people respond to a united and earnest appeal from us? Can we, can they, by any other means, so certainly, or so speedily, assure these vital objects? We can succeed only by concert. It is not "can *any* of us imagine better?" but "can we *all* do better?" The dogmas of the quiet past are inadequate to the stormy present. The occasion is piled high with difficulty, and we must rise with the occasion. As our case is new, so we must think anew and act anew. We must disenthrall ourselves, and then we shall save our country.

"Fellow citizens, we cannot escape history. We, of this Congress and this administration, will be remembered in spite of ourselves. No personal significance, or insignificance, can spare one or another of us. The fiery trial through which we pass will light us down, in honor or dishonor, to the latest generation. We say we are for the Union. The world will not forget that we say this. We know how to save the Union. The world knows we do know how to save it. We — even *we here* — hold the power and bear the responsibility. In *giving* freedom to the *slave*, we *assure* freedom to the *free* — honorable, alike, in what we give and what we preserve. We shall nobly save, or meanly lose, the last best hope of earth. Other means may succeed; this could not fail. The way is plain, peaceful, generous, and just — a way which, if followed, the world will forever applaud, and God must forever bless."[1]

RECONSTRUCTIVE SURGERY
OH, WELL... CLOSE ENOUGH
THE NEW AMERICAN WORK ETHIC...
©1995 WASHINGTON POST WRITERS GROUP 6.29 WILEY

For Those Who Aspire To Greatness...

Conclusion

As we commit ourselves to the pursuit of ethics and character, we must realize this: Two people are now being trained inside each of us. The first is the king or queen we were each made to be. The second is the righteous warrior who lives within. The warrior's role is to beat off everything that would try to keep the king or queen from assuming his or her throne. We must stop anything that would get in the way of our reign in life. To that end, we must guard our pursuit of virtuous character at all costs.

I have heard it said that great men and women do not just happen. It is true — greatness does *not* just happen. There are unseen years of discipline and character development required to equip people for leadership in an hour of need.

During the Second World War, the King of England summoned Winston Churchill to meet with him.

When Churchill stood before the king, the king asked him, "Winston, do you know why I have called you here?"

He said, "No, Your Highness. I have no idea why you have called me here."

The king replied, "Winston, go and form a great, new government."

Winston later related, "In a moment's time, I knew I had been born for that hour. This was the reason I came to this earth. Every moment of my life, up to this time, had only been in preparation for what was about to happen."

Churchill was the Prime Minister of England throughout World War II. During those years, he became one of the greatest and most inspiring leaders of our time. But right after the war ended, Churchill was defeated in an election.

I was watching a documentary about Churchill, awhile back, and a man stated how glad he was that Winston Churchill had been defeated after World War II. I turned and asked someone, whose opinion I hold dear, "Why is it that people didn't care for Winston Churchill after the war?"

My friend responded, "Great men can only be tolerated for short moments in time."

I can see the truth in that statement. The standards of great men are too high for most. What they desire out of life is so great that those who are content with mediocrity can only tolerate them for short spans of time.

The seeds of greatness reside within *you*. However, it is in the times of *preparation* that you build your character and develop your potential for becoming great. *Now* is the time when you must prepare for your hour, whenever that hour may come. **Greatness is planted in the heart of every man, but those who will achieve it are those who realize that time waits for no one.**

It is likely that, for most of us, our hour has not yet come. We haven't yet entered into the ultimate destiny for our lives. But if we are wise, we know that every moment must be invested into preparation for that hour. Every moment, we must get ready. Every moment, we must take it on the chin, if needed, and then rise up again to keep walking in character.

That is our responsibility, our duty, and our honor. Even when we feel like we have been wronged, we must accept the blow or the insult without quitting. We are called to forgive and to walk in compassion, even if we have to do it a thousand times a day. We need to keep developing our character, for our hour *is* coming — the moment when each of us will be called upon to fulfill our purpose on this earth. When that hour comes, we will need every ounce of ethical character we have developed over the years.

So where does that leave us in this present hour? With a very important goal: **Whatever the cost, we must build a character that will last forever.** The outcome of our lives, and the lives of those we love greatly, depends on it!

Appendix I

Leading When I'm Not Sure If I Want To…

What character traits are required for someone in a leadership position? Here are ten qualifications that can guide us:

1. ***A leader must have integrity.*** — In all circumstances, a leader must walk in ethical, honorable conduct that is above reproach or accusation — having nothing in his character, reputation, or example that can be legitimately spoken against.
2. ***A leader must have a stable family life.*** — Regardless of background, it is important for a leader to show commitment to his marriage vows. Marital breakdown is often the result of serious character flaws. Think about it. If a man does not know how to lead and manage his own family, how can he expect to lead others?
3. ***A leader must be faithful.*** — He demonstrates loyalty and commitment to his relationships, whether it is his marriage, his family, his friends, his constituents, or his authorities. Relationship failure is often due to character failure.
4. ***A leader must be sober.*** — The word "sober" means *of a sound mind.* In other words, this leader doesn't go off on little tangents.

Instead, he stays continually on the straight path of wise principle. He consistently sticks to ethically sound beliefs and doesn't waver.

5. ***A leader must be generous.*** — True leaders are given to hospitality, benevolence, and compassion. Regardless of personality traits, they are empathetic, knowing that there is more to life than gathering money, influence, or fame.
6. ***A leader must be able to teach.*** — A leader is not a leader unless he has followers; and followers must be taught.
7. ***A leader must live a self-controlled, exemplary lifestyle.*** — When a person becomes a leader, he finds himself in a position of much greater influence than he previously held. What he does in his life matters to more people than ever before, for he now has a position of authority in their lives.

   A leader completely refrains from any behavior or personal indulgence that could cloud or compromise his judgment. A person who holds the welfare of others in his hands cannot afford the encumbrance of clouded judgment!

   In spite of the personal rights and liberties that he could exercise, a leader will not allow his personal liberty to cause someone else to stumble. He chooses to forego his own liberty, out of a heart motivated by duty and love toward others.
8. ***A leader must be free from greed.*** — His efforts and energies do not revolve around his ability to receive monetary gain from other people. This person is in a leadership position to help others, *not* to satisfy his own appetites. Money isn't the issue for an ethical leader; *people's lives* are the issue.

9. ***A leader must be mature and humble.*** — A young and inexperienced individual who is promoted too quickly will easily become blinded by his own sense of self-importance. This makes him susceptible to making destructive decisions.

10. ***A leader must be respectable.*** — A true leader is respected by the people in his community. A leader who carries no respect also carries no influence; and a leader stripped of influence can benefit no one.

Greater Authority Means Greater Accountability

Although it is good to aspire to authoritative positions, we need to understand this: The higher we go, the more our lives mean to others, and the greater number of people will be affected by our success or failure. Consequently, we must tolerate fewer vices in our own character.

As leaders, we must be determined that those who look to us will never see us fall into compromised character or ill repute. We must live our lives in front of people, not behind them, hiding nothing behind closed doors. This is what each of us must do if we want to be leaders who walk in ethical character. We have to be transparent — quick to tell on ourselves when necessary.

None of us should be willing to fall short in our pursuit of the highest character possible. We each need to be keenly aware of the people who could be adversely affected if we allowed ourselves any slack in our pursuit of excellent character.

We must refuse to become a stumbling block or an obstacle to someone else. We must always remember that what we do *matters* to other people. Therefore, if something we do offends another, we must determine that we will never do it again.

Many people don't really care how others are affected by what they do. They're determined to do what they want, because they are "free moral agents." They don't care if their freedom becomes another man's burden.

But we must understand this truth: The more a person moves into leadership, the less personal freedom he can exercise. The path he walks gets *very narrow!* Why? Because leaders are held to a greater level of accountability. When a person leads, in the lives of others, that person doesn't lead with the freedom to do anything he wants. He is bound to his duty to live a life of discipline and love. He is expected to consider other people in the way he lives his life, for he no longer lives for himself, but for those he serves.

Appendix II

Chapter 1: A Tower Of Strength

- **Character esteems moral strength of greater value than beauty, riches, or fame.**
- **Good character is what others want *you* to possess so they don't have to.**
- **We may not always be rewarded for our strong traits, but we will most definitely be disqualified for the weak ones.**
- **Every breakdown in life can be traced to a failure in character.**
- **Lasting success is inseparably joined to the portrait painted by our character.**
- **No good can come of our future if we refuse to take care of the character flaws that live in the present.**
- **We must never ask questions about tomorrow, if we are not challenging the standards by which we live today.**
- **We must be more interested in improving our own character than in judging the lack of it in others.**
- **If we will not learn when someone instructs us, we will be forced to learn when consequences come to teach us.**
- **Character demonstrates integrity throughout the challenging situations of life.**

Chapter 2: Honor Bound

- Negative attitudes are quickly altered by the self-adjusting person of character.
- Character carries itself with honor through every situation of life.
- Integrity will not always be rewarded BY this life, but integrity will always be rewarded IN this life.
- "Extra-Mile Road" is the boulevard of choice for a person of character.

Chapter 3: Set In Your Ways

- Embracing principle unlocks the door to a safe, secure, and prosperous future.
- Today's excellence is tomorrow's mediocrity.
- Receiving correction cheerfully is a prerequisite for character development.
- We can never change what we are unwilling to face.
- Character does what is right, even in the face of possible rejection.
- If we live by principle, we must never allow ourselves to be affected by the moods and emotions of others.
- Character always chooses to live life by the highest standards.
- The only real goal of life is to become all that we were created to be.

Chapter 4: Facing Your Giants

- Unless we learn to focus on our future, we will be continually tormented by the nightmares of our past.
- If we will choose right character, we will destroy the giant named yesterday.
- We will never perform in a manner that is inconsistent with the way we see ourselves.
- In order to achieve success in the future, one must break the glass ceilings of the past.
- Never attempt to give life to something that should be put to death.
- There is no future in the past.

Chapter 5: You Reap What You Sow

- Embrace ethical principles, even in the face of great opposition.
- Each and every trial we face drives us either closer to or further away from our purpose in life.
- Our lives can beneficially influence others only to the degree that we are willing to walk in nobility of character.
- Good character is not the goal but, rather, the key that unlocks the door to fulfilling life's purpose.
- We will only get out of life what we are willing to put into it.
- Sowing and reaping are the governors of destiny.
- Good character cannot be denied.
- Pursuing excellent character always begins with a decision.

Chapter 6: There Is No Escape

- Today's decisions determine tomorrow's circumstances.
- It is the lack of character that creates the platform for the destruction of intimacy.
- Our commitment to integrity must never be destroyed by our love for another.
- Character pursues doing what is right, not what is comfortable.
- Even when others choose deception, character refuses to compromise truth.
- The seed one sows today is the harvest he will reap tomorrow.
- Refuse to obstruct consequences that come to the life of another.
- When we refuse to learn by instruction, consequences will readily take its place.
- When our entire focus is on getting what we want, we will eventually lose what we had.

Chapter 7: Standing The Test Of Time

- Character refuses to rob its future in order to enjoy its present.
- Character recognizes compliance as an instrument for good in life.
- Character discovers its assignment in every relationship and then postures itself accordingly.
- Character refuses to take authority over something for which it is not responsible.

- When asked to violate principles, character chooses to comply with ethical integrity.
- Submission stops prosecution.
- The fruit of compliance is character; the fruit of character is moral strength; and the effect of moral strength is productivity.
- Character responds to positions of leadership with honor and respect.
- A man of character refuses to circumvent the structure of authority that he has been assigned to obey.
- The choices we make are the only factors that decide whether we will be overtaken with rewards or consequences.
- A person of character views ethical authority as an advocate, sent to do him good.

Chapter 8: Don't Bend The Truth

- Restitution is the most vital ingredient of genuine remorse.
- Restoration is never granted until wrongdoing is fully confronted.
- Confrontation is the final effort to preserve the intimacy of any relationship.
- Truth, in its purest form, can only be defined by a standard far higher than man's.
- Character continually returns to principles of ethics and integrity for its supply of truth.
- Excellence in life can only be achieved when we embrace truth as the only avenue to promotion.

- Character looks to truth to be the most celebrated influencer in its life.
- Character defines itself by continually evaluating its progress in the light of truth.

Pillar 1: Keep Your Cool

- The greatest giant one will ever face is himself.
- One must recognize that his outer flesh and his inner conscience are at odds with one another.
- Whatever we refuse to conquer will ultimately conquer us.
- Character corrects itself so others never have to.
- Self-control begins by recognizing that there is a consequence for every action.
- Tears of sorrow can never wash away the consequence for wrongdoing.
- The proof of authenticity is the willingness to be examined.
- Self-control begins by exposing every thought and feeling to the guidelines of proven principles.

Pillar 2: Don't Bite The Hand That Feeds You

- The refusal to conquer negativity ensures that it will ultimately become our master.
- In the realm of respect or disrespect, there is no middle ground.
- Character continually checks to ensure that its foundation of ethics always exceeds its temptations to compromise.

- Character proves its respect for virtue through its compliance to moral precepts.
- Ethical character bases all of life on the all-encompassing love for truth.
- Accuracy must be continually pursued, in order to protect truth.
- Compliance is not merely a recommendation; it is a requirement.
- Integrity is withheld from anyone who refuses to possess a spirit of compliance.
- Those who esteem character protect and esteem those in positions of authority.
- Leaders aren't looking to measure our maturity; their eyes are fixed on our compliance.

Pillar 3: On The Level

- A person who possesses genuine character aligns his life with the words of his mouth.
- Evasive individuals become agents of destruction when they lie.
- Character seeks to root out every hidden lie that keeps one living in defeat.
- An individual who esteems honesty is willing to speak the truth in love, even when it hurts.
- Character lives a life of truth and sincerity before all men.
- The only person who cannot see a blind spot is the one who has it.

Pillar 4: Find It In Your Heart

- Compassion provides a fresh start to anyone who sincerely commits to the pursuit of change.
- Compassion covets the prize of a tender heart.
- Compassion is willing to put its shoulder under the pain of another, to momentarily lighten the load.
- Compassion is the cloak that character wears during the moments it is relating to a dying world.
- Character demonstrates compassion by actions, for it is hollow when expressed by words alone.
- Acts of kindness are the "get-well cards" left in the hearts of the broken by those who are compassionate.
- If you allow compassion to flow through you, you will discover more compassion within you.
- Character is the recipient of compassion's reward.

Pillar 5: Draw Your Attention

- The game of life is won or lost in the attention to detail.
- Attentiveness ensures that an assignment is completed long before you ever hear the words, "Mission accomplished."
- Promotion is summoned to a person's life the moment he gives attention to detail.
- We won't be rewarded for our similarities to others; rather, we will be rewarded for our differences.

- The foundation of love is honor, and the demonstration of honor is attentiveness.
- True knowledge is gained only by offering someone our full attention.
- Look for the areas where others lack, and then choose to make up the slack.
- In order to bring transformation to this world, every relationship requires the deepest of commitments and consideration.
- Attentiveness is a daily habit that causes us to focus on that which truly matters to others.

Pillar 6: Don't Put Foot In Mouth

- Discretion strategically chooses restraint.
- Discretion is the guard that protects an individual from the calamity of a multitude of words.
- In every situation, discretion knows the attitudes, words, and actions that are right, honorable, and just to act upon.
- Discretion understands that future consequences are the result of present actions.
- Discretion avoids situations that could compromise its commitment to strong moral fortitude.
- Discretion distinguishes right from wrong and then chooses what is right, no matter what the cost.
- It is greater to choose to serve than it is to be approached to serve.
- Character guides its affairs with discretion.
- Discretion celebrates the unequaled value of wisdom.

- Discretion turns knowledge into wise counsel.
- Discretion controls destructive emotions.
- Discretion intuitively knows when to speak and when to be silent.
- Discretion lives in constant preparation for the hour when an honorable purpose summons it to action.

Pillar 7: Bringing It Home

- The proof of ethical character is the development and demonstration of an understanding heart.
- Character strives daily to gain more understanding.
- Reserving judgment for the appropriate time clothes a man with understanding.
- Understanding willingly accepts responsibility for its behavior.
- Our value to others is in direct proportion to the problems we are willing to solve for them.
- We will only be remembered for the problems we have solved or the problems we have caused.
- It is impossible to be noncompliant and still become victorious over the challenges in life.
- Understanding distinguishes and follows the right path in any situation.
- Understanding ensures that the voice of principle means more than the voice of excuse.

- **A person of understanding is continually built up, refreshed, and renewed by the wellspring of his virtuous life.**
- **Understanding refuses to participate in any endeavor that promises future regret.**

For Those Who Aspire To Greatness

- **Greatness is planted in the heart of every man, but those who will achieve it are those who realize that time waits for no one.**

Appendix III

Words To Live By

Character is like a tree and reputation like its shadow. The shadow is what we think of it; the tree is the real thing. — *Abraham Lincoln*

More men fail through lack of purpose than through lack of talent. — *Billy Sunday*

Great minds have purposes. Others have wishes. — *Washington Irving*

What comes out of you when you are squeezed is what is inside you. — *Wayne Dyer*

The superior man is modest in his speech, but exceeds in his actions. — *Confucius*

An unused life is an early death. — *Unknown*

Purpose is the engine, the power that drives and directs our lives. — *John R. Noe*

Most time is wasted not in hours but in minutes. A bucket with a small hole in the bottom gets just as empty as a bucket that is deliberately emptied. — *Paul J. Meyer*

Men decide their habits; their habits decide their future.
— *Mike Murdock*

Sow an action and you reap a habit; sow a habit and you reap character; sow character and you reap a destiny. — *Charles Reade*

God does not give you integrity; rather, you develop it, cultivate it, seek it out, and chisel it out from the granite of your being. — *Unknown*

Talent without discipline is like an octopus on roller skates. There is plenty of movement, but you never know if it's going forward, sideways, or backwards. — *H. Jackson Brown*

My outward actions are little more than my inner convictions.
— *Robb Thompson*

Never complain about what you permit. — *Mike Murdock*

Life is a grindstone. Whether it grinds you down or polishes you depends on what you are made of. — *Unknown*

The true test of a servant is if I act like one when I am treated like one.
— *Bill Gothard*

To be right too soon is to be wrong. — *Emperor Hardin*

Believability is more than mere words; it is the integrity of the individual.
— *Ed Cole*

The measure of success is not whether you have a tough problem to deal with but whether it's the same one you had last year. — *Former Secretary of State John Dulles*

The absence of character is often more visible than its presence. — *Unknown*

What we do on some great occasion will probably depend on what we already are; and what we will be is a result of previous years of self-discipline. — *Oxford University Professor H.P Liddon*

Leadership is the potent combination of strategy and character. But if you must be without one, be without strategy. — *General Norman Schwarzkopf*

When one has integrity, there is an absence of hypocrisy. He or she is personally reliable, financially accountable, and privately clean...innocent of impure motives. — *Charles Swindoll*

Power is like a mighty river. As long as it keeps its course, it is a useful thing of beauty. But when it floods its banks, it brings a great destruction. — *John Maxwell*

Money doesn't change men; it merely unmasks them. If a man is naturally selfish or arrogant or greedy, the money brings that out; that is all. — *Henry Ford*

There is no dignity quite so impressive and no independence quite so important as living within your means. — *President Calvin Coolidge*

Principles should not change with time or polls.
— *President George W. Bush*

There are two kinds of people who never achieve much in their lifetime: the person who won't do what he is told and the one who does no more than he is told. — *Andrew Carnegie*

Excellence is doing a common thing in an uncommon way.
— *Booker T. Washington*

People forget how fast you did a job, but always remember how well you did it. — *Howard W. Newton*

Don't be afraid to give up the good for the great. — *Kenny Rogers*

The quality of a person's life is in direct proportion to his commitment to excellence, regardless of his chosen field of endeavor.
— *Vince Lombardi*

Always do more than is required of you. — *General George S. Patton*

Superiority is doing things a little better than anybody else can do them.
— *Orison Swelt Marden*

We are judged by what we finish, not by what we start. — *Unknown*

The only thing that walks back from the tomb with the mourners and refuses to be buried is the character of a man... What a man is survives him. It can never be buried. — *J. R. Miller*

Notes

Notes

Grateful acknowledgment is made for the use of the following material.

Chapter 1

1. Thomas J. Stanley, *The Millionaire Mind* (Kansas City, MO: Andrews McMeel Publishing, 2000), p. 250-251.

Chapter 5

1. Arthur S. DeMoss, *The Rebirth of America* (Philadelphia, PA: Arthur S. DeMoss Foundation, 1986), p. 141.
2. Based on accumulative data from the two primary sources of U.S. abortion statistics (Centers for Disease Control and Alan Guttmacher Institute).

Chapter 6

1. Denny Kenaston, *The Pursuit of Godly Seed* (Reamstown, PA: Home Fires Publishers, 2003), p. 62.

2. Psalm 55:9-11, *New Living Translation (NLT) Holy Bible. New Living Translation* copyright © 1996, 2004 by Tyndale Charitable Trust. Used by permission of Tyndale House Publishers, Inc., Wheaton, IL 60189. All rights reserved.
3. Ibid. Psalm 55:12-14, 20-21, *NLT.*

Chapter 9

1. Robb Thompson, *Everyday Ways to Enjoy Success at Work* (Chicago, IL: Family Harvest Church, 2006), p. 55.

Chapter 10

1. Al Covino, "A True Story of Integrity," *Sacred Hoops,* http://www.sacredhoops.com/famous-sport-quote-a-true-story-on-integrity/ (Nov. 22, 2010).

Chapter 11

1. Author Unknown, "The Emperor's Seed," *After Hours Inspirational Stories,* http://www.inspirationalstories.com/5/524.html (Nov. 22, 2010).

Chapter 12

1. Job 29:12-16, *New King James Version,* copyright © 1982 by Thomas Nelson, Inc., Nashville, Tennessee. All rights reserved.
2. Ibid. Psalm 35:13-14, *NKJV.*

3. Kelsey Tyler, "A Football Hero in Street Clothes," *The Hidden Hand of God: Extraordinary Escapes and Rescues* (Carmel, NY: Guideposts, 2002), p. 141.
4. Kathy Pinto, "The Grandfather's Table," *Inspirational Christian Stories and Poems,* http://www.inspirationalarchive.com/texts/topics/compassion/grandfatherstable.shtml (Nov. 22, 2010).

Chapter 13

1. Author Unknown, "God's Purpose in Things," *Sky Writing,* http://www.skywriting.net/inspirational/stories/gods_purpose_in_things.html (Nov. 22, 2010).

Chapter 14

1. Proverbs 5:1-4, *NKJV.*
2. Robb Thompson, *Everyday Ways to Enjoy Success at Work* (Chicago, IL: Family Harvest Church, 2006), p. 103.

Chapter 15

1. Abraham Lincoln, edited by Roy P. Basler, "Annual Message to Congress – Concluding Remarks," *Abraham Lincoln Online,* http://showcase.netins.net/web/creative/lincoln/speeches/congress.htm (Nov. 22, 2010).

Prayer of Salvation

God loves you—no matter who you are, no matter what your past. God loves you so much that He gave His one and only begotten Son for you. The Bible tells us that "...whoever believes in him shall not perish but have eternal life" (John 3:16 NIV). Jesus laid down His life and rose again so we could spend eternity with Him in heaven and experience His absolute best on earth. If you would like to receive Jesus into your life, say the following prayer out loud and mean it from your heart.

Heavenly Father, I come to You admitting that I am a sinner. Right now, I choose to turn away from sin, and I ask You to cleanse me of all unrighteousness. I believe that Your Son, Jesus, died on the cross to take away my sins. I also believe that He rose again from the dead so that I might be forgiven of my sins and made righteous through faith in Him. I call upon the name of Jesus Christ to be the Savior and Lord of my life. Jesus, I choose to follow You and ask that You fill me with the power of the Holy Spirit. I declare that right now I am a child of God. I am free from sin and full of the righteousness of God. I am saved in Jesus' name. Amen.

If you prayed this prayer to receive Jesus Christ as your Savior for the first time, please contact us on the Web at **harrisonhouse.com** to receive a free book.

Or you may write to us at

Harrison House

P.O. Box 35035

Tulsa, OK 74153

The Harrison House Vision

Proclaiming the truth and the power

Of the Gospel of Jesus Christ

With excellence;

Challenging Christians to

Live victoriously,

Grow spiritually,

Know God intimately.